ON ROMANS

ON ROMANS

and Other
New Testament Essays

C. E. B. CRANFIELD

Emeritus Professor of Theology
University of Durham

T&T CLARK
A Continuum imprint
LONDON • NEW YORK

T&T CLARK LTD

A Continuum imprint

59 George Street	370 Lexington Avenue
Edinburgh EH2 2LQ	New York 10017–6503
Scotland	USA
www.tandtclark.co.uk	www.continuumbooks.com

First published 1998
Reprinted 2002

ISBN 0 567 08624 0 HB
ISBN 0 567 08637 2 PB

British Library Cataloguing-in-Publication Data
A catalogue record for this book is available from the British Library

Typeset by Waverley Typesetters, Galashiels
Printed and bound in Great Britain by Bookcraft Ltd, Avon

To Ruth, Mary and Elisabeth

Contents

Preface

For permission to include in this collection of essays material which has already been published elsewhere grateful acknowledgement is made to the editors and publishers of the following journals: *The Expository Times, Irish Biblical Studies, Journal for the Study of the New Testament, Metanoia, Reformed Review, Scottish Journal of Theology*; and to Professor L. D. Hurst, The Very Reverend Dr N. T. Wright and the Oxford University Press.

My indebtedness to my wife for her constant help and unfailing patience and for much more besides and to my two daughters for the encouragement which they are to me is greater than I can express.

Durham, December 1997   C.E.B.C.

1

'The Works of the Law' in the Epistle to the Romans

The particular concern of this essay* is Professor J. D. G. Dunn's understanding of Paul's use of the phrase ἔργα νόμου in Romans, as expounded in his commentary[1] and in several other recent works.[2] It is an understanding which is to a large extent determinative of his view of the Epistle as a whole, and it is an understanding to which he has apparently come, at least in part, under the stimulation of Professor E. P. Sanders' work, although in his understanding of the phrase he actually disagrees with him.

It is Professor Dunn's contention that Paul has been mis-understood by successive generations of commentators. By 'the works of the law', which he describes as 'a key phrase whose importance for understanding Paul's thought in this letter can hardly be overestimated',[3] Paul did not mean obedience to the law generally, but specifically, he thinks, adherence to those practices prescribed by the law which most obviously distinguished Jews from their Gentile neighbours, in particular circumcision, keeping the sabbath and observance of the food laws; and, when Paul declared that no flesh will be justified before God by the works of

---

* First published in *Journal for the Study of the New Testament* 43 (1991), pp. 89–101.

[1] *Romans* (Word Biblical Commentary), 2 volumes, Dallas, 1988.
[2] E.g. 'The New Perspective on Paul' (Manson Memorial Lecture, 1982), in *BJRL* 65.2 (1983), pp. 95–122; 'Works of the Law and the Curse of the Law (Galatians 3.10–14)', in *NTS* 31 (1985), pp. 523–42.
[3] *Romans*, p. 158.

the law, he did not mean that no one will be justified on the ground of his having obeyed the law since fallen men and women come nowhere near such true obedience, but was polemicizing against his Jewish contemporaries' complacent reliance on their privileged status as God's covenant people and their exclusiveness towards the Gentiles.[4]

I feel obliged to question this view; but, in so doing I wish to acknowledge that Professor Dunn has put all students of Romans greatly in his debt by giving them so rich an abundance of detailed and suggestive exegesis, including many fresh and stimulating insights. Even where we are not convinced by him, he does us the very valuable service of forcing us to re-examine the text strenuously and to re-think matters we have tended to take for granted and of helping us to look at key points in the Epistle from new angles. It is a commentary with which we shall have to reckon and from which we shall be learning for a long time to come.

Some facts about word-use may be noted at this point. The phrase ἔργα νόμου occurs twice in Romans (three times in the Textus Receptus: it has it in 9.32), six times in Galatians, and nowhere else in the New Testament. In addition, the singular τὸ ἔργον τοῦ νόμου occurs once in Romans. Both ἔργον and νόμος are common words in the New Testament. According to the frequency table in Kurt Aland's *Vollständige Konkordanz zum griechischen Neuen Testament*,[5] ἔργον is the twenty-sixth most common noun in the Greek New Testament, occurring 169 times, sixty-eight in the Pauline corpus and fifteen in Romans; and νόμος is the nineteenth most common noun, occurring 195 times, 121 in the Pauline corpus and seventy-four in Romans.

Since six out of the eight occurrences of ἔργα νόμου in the New Testament are to be found in chapters 2 and 3 of Galatians and since Galatians was written before Romans, no one who is concerned with Paul's use of the phrase in Romans can afford simply to ignore the evidence of Galatians. So, before we turn to our special task, we must look briefly at ἔργα νόμου in Galatians.

[4] *Romans*, pp. 153–5, 158–9.
[5] Band II, Berlin and New York, 1978, p. 407.

In his 1982 Manson Memorial Lecture, 'The New Perspective on Paul', Professor Dunn concentrated on Galatians 2.16 (in the English Revised Version: 'yet knowing that a man is not justified by the works of the law, save through faith in Jesus Christ, even we believed on Christ Jesus, that we might be justified by faith in Christ, and not by the works of the law: because by the works of the law shall no flesh be justified'). Dunn argued that the context justifies the inference that by 'the works of the law' here Paul meant such things as circumcision and the observance of the food laws, and these things as characteristically and distinctively Jewish.[6] He maintains that they were understood neither by Paul's Jewish interlocutors nor by Paul himself

> as works which *earn* God's favour, as merit-amassing observances. They are rather seen as *badges*: they are simply what membership of the covenant people involves, what mark out the Jews as God's people . . . In other words, Paul has in view precisely what Sanders calls 'covenantal nomism'. And what he denies is . . . that God's grace extends only to those who wear the badge of the covenant . . . The phrase 'works of the law' in Gal. 2.16 is, in fact, a fairly restricted one: it refers precisely to these same identity markers described above . . . those regulations prescribed by the law which any good Jew would simply take for granted to describe what a good Jew did.[7]

A similar explanation of the other three occurrences of ἔργα νόμου in Galatians (in 3.2, 5 and 10) is given in his *New Testament Studies* article, 'Works of the Law and the Curse of the Law (Gal. 3.10–14)'.[8]

I think it should be admitted that as far as Galatians is concerned, Dunn's explanation of ἔργα νόμου does have a certain plausibility. The fact that the occasion of the letter was Paul's having received news of the activities of people who were insisting on the need for Gentiles who had accepted the gospel to be circumcised; the prominence of references to circumcision (περιτέμνειν occurs six times, περιτομή seven times,

---

[6] 'New Perspective', p. 107.
[7] 'New Perspective', pp. 110–11.
[8] 'Works of the Law', pp. 532–5.

ἀκροβυστία three times); the presence of expressions like ὁ Ἰουδαϊσμός in 1.13, 14, αἱ πατρικαί μου παραδόσεις in 1.14, μετὰ τῶν ἐθνῶν συνεσθίειν in 2.12, ἐθνικῶς καὶ οὐχὶ Ἰουδαϊκῶς ζῆν and ἰουδαΐζειν in 2.14; perhaps even the occurrence of ἔργα νόμου six times in the space of sixteen verses itself – these things might seem to be some support for understanding ἔργα νόμου in Galatians in Dunn's 'restricted' sense.

But none of them, nor yet any of the other points which, to my knowledge, have been urged in favour of the restricted sense, would seem to be decisive, and, in the absence of any clear indication that ἔργα νόμου has a special restricted sense, the balance of probability must, I think, be on the side of taking it in what is surely the natural sense of the phrase as a Greek phrase. Moreover, on the assumption that it is used in the sense of '(doing) the works which the law requires', 'obedience to the law', an exegesis of all the verses in which it occurs, which does justice to their context and to the rest of the letter, is possible. By contrast, Dunn's exegesis in the latter part of his *New Testament Studies* article, which strikes one as unconscionably tortuous, reaches a climax in its attribution to Paul of a narrow view of what Christ accomplished by his death (e.g. 'The curse which was removed therefore by Christ's death was the curse which had previously prevented that blessing [i.e. the covenant blessing] from reaching the Gentiles, the curse of a wrong understanding of the law'[9] and 'In his earliest extant teaching on the death of Jesus he asserts that the whole point of Jesus' death on the cross was to remove the boundary of the law and its consequent curse, to liberate the blessing promised to Abraham for all to enjoy'),[10] which surely sorts extremely ill with the sense of deep personal indebtedness expressed in 2.20 ('. . . *the faith* which is in the Son of God, who loved me, and gave himself up for me').

While some features of Galatians do lend to Dunn's explanation of ἔργα νόμου a certain plausibility as far as its occurrences in

[9] 'Works of the Law', p. 536.
[10] 'Works of the Law', p. 539.

that epistle are concerned, it is very much more probable that in Galatians the phrase has its natural general sense. The facts that both ἔργον and νόμος are very common words in the New Testament (as we saw above) and that the combination of ἔργα with νόμος in the genitive is a very natural formation seem to make it extremely unlikely that Paul would use ἔργα νόμου in a special restricted sense without giving a clear indication that he was doing so. Dunn's idea that the phrase (in the restricted sense he gives it) was 'either already familiar to his [i.e. Paul's] readers or self-evident to them in its significance'[11] is, in my view, quite unconvincing.[12] But, even if Dunn's explanation of ἔργα νόμου in Galatians were accepted, the meaning of the phrase in Romans would not have been settled. Paul could scarcely assume that the Christians in Rome would be familiar with what he had written to the Galatians. That Paul was capable of using the same expression in different senses on different occasions is clear enough.

We turn now at last to Romans. The first occurrence of ἔργα νόμου is in 3.20: διότι ἐξ ἔργων νόμου οὐ δικαιωθήσεται πᾶσα σὰρξ ἐνώπιον αὐτοῦ, διὰ γὰρ νόμου ἐπίγνωσις ἁμαρτίας. Dunn explains ἔργα νόμου here as meaning quite specifically those observances like circumcision and keeping of the food laws 'which marked the Jews off from the other nations as distinctively God's people'.[13]

But there are several compelling reasons why this explanation must be rejected.

1. It fails to take account of the fact that 3.20 stands in relation to the whole argument from 1.18 on. When Dunn says of 3.20, 'The concluding summary of the first main stage of the argument must refer back to what Paul had been attacking for the last chapter and a half, particularly Jewish pride in the law, and especially in circumcision as the most fundamental distinctive marker of the

---

[11] 'Works of the Law', p. 527.

[12] The passages in the Qumran texts, to which he appeals in 'Works of the Law', p. 528; *Romans*, p. 154, do not seem to me to offer very clear support.

[13] *Romans*, p. 155.

people of the law',[14] he has lost sight of Paul's argument. He should have referred back not just one and a half chapters, but right back to 1.18 where this section begins. Paul's concern from 1.18 on has surely been to lead up to the conclusion expressed in 3.20a and then restated in the opening lines of the next section in 3.23 (RV: 'For all have sinned, and fall short of the glory of God'), namely, that all human beings are sinners (Jesus Christ alone excepted) whose only possibility of being righteous before God is by God's free gift accepted in faith; and his concern in 2.1–3.19 is not primarily to polemicize against Jews (Dunn speaks of 'Paul's polemic here'),[15] but rather to draw out the full meaning of 1.18–32 by demonstrating that there are no exceptions to its sweeping judgment – even the Jews who might not without reason think of themselves as superior to the pagan world around are no exception.

2. It is surely ruled out by the presence of the latter part of 3.20. The force of γάϱ at the beginning of διὰ γὰϱ νόμου ἐπίγνωσις ἁμαρτίας is ignored by Dunn, though he correctly translates it by 'for'. It indicates that this sentence is added as support for what has just been said. But, while a statement that the effect of the law is actually to show up human sin does indeed support what has been said in the first part of the verse, if in that first part 'the works of the law' means obedience to the law generally, it is difficult to see how it is support for it, if 'the works of the law' has Dunn's 'restricted sense', and his explanation would involve supposing an awkward change in the way the law is being thought of between the two parts of the verse.

3. It involves taking the plural ἔϱγα νόμου in a quite different sense from that of the singular τὸ ἔϱγον τοῦ νόμου in 2.15. While this is not impossible (for Paul, we know, can use the same word in different senses), it is surely preferable, if possible, to take it in the same or a closely related sense, unless the context forbids this. I understand τὸ ἔϱγον τοῦ νόμου in 2.15 as 'the work which the law requires', and take Paul's meaning here to be that the eschatological promise of Jeremiah 31.33 that God would write his

[14] *Romans*, p. 154.
[15] *Romans*, p. 154.

6

law in the hearts of his people is being fulfilled in the Gentiles who have believed in Christ. The use of the singular 'may be explained as intended to bring out the essential unity of the law's requirements, the fact that the plurality of commandments is no confused and confusing conglomeration but a recognizable and intelligible whole'[16] (cf. the use of τὸ δικαίωμα in 8.4 and the replacement of 'the works of God' in John 6.28 by 'the work of God' in the following verse). It seems to me that 2.15 tells in favour of taking ἔργα νόμου in 3.20 in the general sense rather than in Dunn's restricted sense. The difference then between 'work' in 2.15 and 'work' in 3.20 will simply be that in the former place it denotes the work *as prescribed*, in the latter the work *as actually done*. And if the Gentiles referred to are taken to be pagan Gentiles, it is equally impossible to give to 'the work of the law' anything like Dunn's restricted sense.

4. Dunn's explanation is further called in question by the occurrence in Romans of such expressions as οἱ ποιηταὶ νόμου in 2.13; τὰ τοῦ νόμου ποιεῖν in 2.14; νόμον πράσσειν in 2.25; τὰ δικαιώματα τοῦ νόμου φυλάσσειν in 2.26; τὸν νόμον τελεῖν in 2.27; δουλεύειν νόμῳ θεοῦ in 7.25; τὸ δικαίωμα τοῦ νόμου πληροῦν in 8.4; and νόμον πληροῦν in 13.8. All these are, it seems to me, naturally connected with the phrase ἔργα νόμου. In none of the occurrences of these expressions in Romans is it at all feasible to see a reference to circumcision, etc. (Dunn's proposed restricted sense of ἔργα νόμου): in 2.25 circumcision is explicitly contrasted with practising the law.

5. It is also called in question by what we find when we look at the occurrences in Romans of ἔργον and νόμος in separation. In seven out of the twelve occurrences of ἔργον without νόμου, it clearly does not refer to such things as circumcision (the other five we shall consider below). With regard to νόμος, it would surely be difficult for even the most ardent champion of 'the new look on Romans', after a survey of the more than seventy occurrences of νόμος in the Epistle, to deny that, when Paul uses

[16] C. E. B. Cranfield, *A Critical and Exegetical Commentary on the Epistle to the Romans* 1, Edinburgh, [6]1987, p. 158.

the word νόμος, it is the law in its fundamental theological and ethical character which he normally has in mind, not the law as providing an obvious national identity-marker distinguishing Jews from Gentiles.

6. Possibly we should see a sixth reason for rejecting Dunn's explanation in the fact that in 14.1–15.13, a section which may perhaps reflect Paul's knowledge of actual problems confronting the Roman Christians, it is to 'the strong' and not to 'the weak' that the main thrust of Paul's exhortation is directed. Would one not expect it to be otherwise, if Dunn's view were right? If Paul really was as much preoccupied with polemic against Jewish reliance on circumcision and the observance of the food-laws and the sabbath as Dunn seems to think, is it likely that he would have weighted his exhortation in this section in the way he has? (I assume that 'the weak' are Christians, mostly Jewish, whose faith has not yet given them the freedom enjoyed by 'the strong' and who still feel obliged, as believers in Christ, to observe the ceremonial law.)

In view of what has been said above, the conclusion seems to me inevitable that Dunn's interpretation of 3.20 must be rejected. The meaning of 3.20 is surely, as others have long recognized, that justification before God on the ground of one's obedience to the law is not a possibility for fallen human beings, since none of them is righteous and the effect of the law is to show up their sin as sin and themselves as sinners.

We turn next to the other occurrence in Romans of ἔργα νόμου in 3.28 (λογιζόμεθα γὰρ δικαιοῦσθαι πίστει ἄνθρωπον χωρὶς ἔργων νόμου). Dunn understands it as in 3.20, and he heads the section 3.27–31, 'The Consequences for the Self-Understanding of the Jewish People'. Though this may fit in well with his view of Paul's argument so far, it seems to me to be a quite unjustified limiting of Paul's concern. How could Paul, immediately after vv. 21–26, verses which repeat the conclusion of the whole argument from 1.18 to 3.20 by the statement that all have sinned and lack the glory of God, and proclaim solemnly and directly the redemption in Christ Jesus and God's costly forgiveness, go on merely to draw out the consequences for the self-understanding of the Jewish people? At this particular point anything less than a drawing-out of the consequences for the self-understanding of human beings as such would surely be an intolerable anticlimax. It is not just Jewish boasting which is here excluded (*pace* a good many commentators), but all human boasting before God. That ἔργα νόμου must have the same sense here as it has in 3.20 can hardly be denied. If any human beings at all are justified, it must be without their having obeyed the law, since all are sinners who lack the glory of God. (Verses 29 and 30 [RV 'Or is God *the God* of Jews only? is he not *the God* of Gentiles also? Yea, of Gentiles also: if so be that God is one, and he shall justify the circumcision by faith, and the uncircumcision through faith'], referring as they do to the distinction between Jews and Gentiles, might at first sight seem to be support for Dunn's view that this section is intended as polemic against Jewish pride in such identity-markers as circumcision. But I take it that the function of those two verses is to support v. 28 by indicating that to deny its truth and to claim that men actually earn justification by their obedience to the law would be to imply something obviously false, namely, that God is not the God of all men but only of the Jews. God's ultimate impartiality is shown by the fact that he will justify Jew and Gentile alike by or through faith, that is, by undeserved grace.)

We must now turn our attention to several places in which ἔργα occurs without νόμου but apparently with a similar sense to that of ἔργα νόμου. The first two of these are in Romans 4. With reference to 4.2 (εἰ γὰρ Ἀβραὰμ ἐξ ἔργων ἐδικαιώθη, ἔχει καύχημα, ἀλλ᾽ οὐ πρὸς θεόν), Dunn insists that ἐξ ἔργων 'should not be taken as a more generalized statement than ἐξ ἔργων νόμου, as the parallel with 3.20 and the similar usage in 3.27–28 clearly indicate',[17] and that 'The recurrence of the key themes, "works" and "boasting", indicates clearly that Paul once again is thinking of the typical national confidence of his own people as to their election by God and privileged position under the law'.[18] With reference to 4.6 (καθάπερ καὶ Δαυὶδ λέγει τὸν

---

[17] *Romans*, p. 200.
[18] *Romans*, p. 227.

μακαρισμὸν τοῦ ἀνθρώπου ᾧ ὁ θεὸς λογίζεται δικαιοσύνην χωρὶς ἔργων), he claims that what is meant by ἔργα is 'the sort of nomistic service in which the devout Jew could boast'.[19] But, in reply it must be said that:

(i) 'him that justifieth the ungodly' in v. 5 strongly suggests that Abraham's lack of works is thought of as having a moral content;

(ii) the quotation of Psalm 32 in vv. 7 and 8 supports taking 'works' in a general, rather than in Dunn's 'restricted', sense, since it identifies being justified apart from works with having sins forgiven;

(iii) vv. 14 and 15 would seem also to weigh against taking ἔργα in Dunn's narrow sense, since the point of those verses seems to be that the possibility of justification through the law is not open, since all are sinners incapable of fulfilling its requirements; and

(iv) the position of chapter 4 in the ongoing argument of Romans requires that ἔργα here should be taken in the general sense, if what we have said in connection with 3.20 and 28 was correct.

The next occurrence of ἔργα to be considered is in 9.11–12 (μήπω γὰρ γεννηθέντων μηδὲ πραξάντων τι ἀγαθὸν ἢ φαῦλον, ἵνα ἡ κατ᾽ ἐκλογὴν πρόθεσις τοῦ θεοῦ μένῃ, οὐκ ἐξ ἔργων ἀλλ᾽ ἐκ τοῦ καλοῦντος, ἐρρέθη αὐτῇ ὅτι ὁ μείζων δουλεύσει τῷ ἐλάσσονι). Again Dunn insists on taking ἔργα in his restricted sense. He says, for example, 'In particular Paul is concerned to demonstrate that his fellow Jews should not attempt to understand Israel's election in terms of law keeping. Israel's selection took place before his birth and therefore neither depends on, nor can be characterized by such distinctive Jewish "works of the law" as circumcision and observance of food laws, sabbath, and feast days.'[20] But in that case, why did Paul write 'neither having done anything good or bad', which would seem to imply that the 'works' referred to must have a moral content?

[19] *Romans*, p. 206.
[20] *Romans*, p. 549.

The fourth of these occurrences of ἔργα is in 9.32, in which Paul gives as the reason why Israel, which was pursuing the law of· righteousness, has not attained to it, the fact that they pursued it not on the basis of faith but as on the basis of works (οὐκ ἐκ πίστεως ἀλλ' ὡς ἐξ ἔργων). Dunn rejects the view that Paul means by pursuit of the law ὡς ἐξ ἔργων the illusory attempt to come to terms with it on the basis of one's deserving, the cherishing of the notion that one can so adequately fulfil its demands as to put God in one's debt. Rather, it was understanding 'the law defining righteousness . . . too narrowly in terms of the requirements of the law which mark off Jew from Gentile'.[21] And some pages later he says: 'Israel's mistake was not that they had understood righteousness as obedience to the law . . . , but that they had understood obedience to the law too much in terms of specific acts of obedience like circumcision, sabbath observance, and ritual purity . . . they had treated the law and the righteousness it requires at too superficial and too nationalistic a level. . .'.[22] Congruously with this understanding of 9.32, he takes τὴν ἰδίαν [δικαιοσύνην] in 10.3 to mean 'their own [righteousness]', not as attained by their own efforts but as peculiar to them to the exclusion of the Gentiles.[23] But, with God's righteousness mentioned twice in the verse, it is surely putting too great a strain on credulity to suggest that a contrast between God's righteousness and their own was not intended; and, if that was intended, it is hard to resist the conclusion that the contrast is between the status of righteousness before God which is God's gift and a status earned for themselves. It seems to us that 10.3 is strong support for the view of ὡς ἐξ ἔργων in 9.32, which Dunn rejects.

The last of the occurrences of ἔργα to be considered is in 11.6. Paul has just said that at the present time there is a remnant according to the election of grace, and he continues: εἰ δὲ χάριτι, οὐκέτι ἐξ ἔργων, ἐπεὶ ἡ χάρις οὐκέτι γίνεται χάρις. Once more Dunn is very confident of the rightness of his interpretation. 'ἐξ

---

[21] *Romans*, p. 582.
[22] *Romans*, p. 593.
[23] *Romans*, p. 587.

ἔργων is, of course, short for ἐξ ἔργων νόμου . . . The point is polemical . . . [The "works" are] "works" understood as the hallmark of election, as that which marks out the elect as such . . . the New Jerusalem Bible's rendering of ἔργα as "good actions" perpetuates the classic misunderstanding that Paul is objecting to a belief that justification can be earned by good works . . .'.[24] And again a few pages later he underlines the identification of the works referred to with 'the national customs and ritual acts which defined their identity as God's holy people, both ethnically and religiously (circumcision, sabbath, food laws, etc.)'.[25] But has not Dunn lost sight of Paul's actual argument here? In 11.2b–10 Paul is concerned to make the point that not all of Israel is unbelieving. As in Elijah's time there were the mysterious seven thousand who had not bowed their knees to Baal, so now too there is a remnant – the Jewish Christians. And, as it was in Elijah's day, so now also it is by God's election of grace that a remnant exists. And, if it is by grace that a remnant consisting of the Jewish Christians exists, then it is not on the ground of their ἔργα. But Paul's purpose in the whole section 11.1–36 is to support the theme stated in 11.2a (God has not cast off his people which he foreknew) and to suggest strongly that there is hope for those who at present are unbelieving. The fact that there are some Jewish Christians now is a sign of hope with regard to the still unbelieving Jews. In this context then a statement that the present remnant's existence stems from God's grace and not from the remnant's works in the sense of their having obeyed the law makes good sense, as it suggests there is hope for still unbelieving Israel which also lacks works in this sense; but a statement that the remnant's existence stems from God's grace and not from its works in the sense of loyalty to circumcision, food laws, etc. does not in this context make such good sense, since unbelieving Israel has such works in abundance. In this context one would expect ἔργα to denote something which both the members of the remnant and also unbelieving Israel alike lack.

---

[24] *Romans*, p. 639.
[25] *Romans*, p. 647.

The foregoing exegetical discussion has shown, I think, that Professor Dunn's explanation of ἔργα νόμου in Romans (and also of ἔργα alone where it seems to be equivalent to ἔργα νόμου) as referring specifically to those practices which function as identity-markers, distinguishing Jews from their Gentile neighbours, in particular, circumcision, observance of the sabbath and observance of food laws, must be rejected; and that even in Galatians, where at first sight it might seem to possess a certain plausibility, his explanation of ἔργα νόμου should be rejected.

I do not dispute his often-repeated description of the attitude of the typical Jew of Paul's time. I regard it as highly likely that Paul's Jewish contemporaries were indeed liable to be specially preoccupied with those practices of the law which most obviously expressed and safeguarded Israel's distinctiveness, to be complacently reliant on their nation's privileged position as God's chosen people, and to cherish a proud exclusiveness towards those beyond its boundaries. I accept too that Paul, committed as he was to the Gentile mission, must have disapproved of such an attitude. But I am certainly not convinced that Paul was as preoccupied with polemic against this Jewish attitude as Professor Dunn makes out. His view seems to me to do less than justice both to the all-important christological dimension of Paul's criticism of his Jewish contemporaries (see, for example, Rom. 9.32b–33) and also to the clarity and steadiness of his vision of the situation of human beings as such in the light of the gospel. In so far as it actually reduces Paul's argument to polemic against a misunderstanding probably not shared by the majority of those he was addressing (not to mention Christians of today), would it perhaps be fair to say that its effect is a weakening of the impact of the Epistle – a blunting of its cutting edge, a giving the impression that it is less pointedly relevant to human life than it really is?

To conclude, I submit that the explanation of ἔργα νόμου in Romans rejected by Professor Dunn is the true explanation, namely, that it denotes (the doing of) the works which the law requires, obedience to the law; and that, when Paul says that no human being will be justified in God's sight by works of the law, he means that no one will earn a status of righteousness before

God by obedience to the law, because such true obedience is not forthcoming from fallen human beings. The statement that God saved Christians 'not by works *done* in righteousness, which we did ourselves, but according to his mercy' and the description of their destiny as 'being justified by his grace' are (whoever actually composed Tit. 3.4ff) true to Paul's mind and provide a helpful commentary on Paul's use of ἔργα νόμου in Romans. It should, of course, go without saying that Paul *also* believed that *there is a sense* in which the righteous requirement of the law is being fulfilled in the believer (Rom. 8.4), that there is something which may be called 'fulfilment of the law', which is no full or perfect obedience and in no way establishes a claim on God, but is simply that humble faith in God's grace, penitence for one's deep sinfulness, past and continuing, and a beginning of being at least turned in the direction of obedience to God, which the Holy Spirit works in the believer.

2

A Note on Romans 5.20–21

That Romans 5.20–1 is a difficult passage has long been recognized. It forms the conclusion of the paragraph 5.12–21, the main feature of which is the comparison between Christ and Adam. From ancient times there has been wide agreement that in v. 12 Paul, having started on his comparison, breaks off (v. 12b being not the expected apodosis but a continuation of the protasis),[1] in order first to justify his use of the verb ἁμαρτάνειν in v. 12b, which in view of 3.20b and 4.15b might seem problematic, and secondly to make it absolutely clear, before his comparison has been completed (though the last five words of v. 14 are a strong hint of what it is going to be), that in every particular except for the one point of comparison the two persons compared are altogether dissimilar. Then in v. 18 he at last states the comparison, v. 18a repeating the substance of v. 12 in a different and highly condensed form and v. 18b giving the long-expected completion. Verse 19 then supports and elucidates v. 18. Verses 20–21 bring the paragraph to a close by referring to the part played by the law, a subject already touched on in vv. 13–14.

1. The first matter to be considered is παρεισῆλθεν. It has often been assumed that it must carry a more or less depreciatory sense. Thus, for example, Sanday and Headlam paraphrase: 'Then Law came in, as a sort of "afterthought", a secondary and subordinate stage, in the Divine plan',[2] and Barrett translates:

[1] Though this has been challenged by C. K. Barrett and others, and in the 2nd edition of his commentary (*The Epistle to the Romans*, London, 1991, pp. 101, 103–4) he still maintains his interpretation.
[2] *A Critical and Exegetical Commentary on the Epistle to the Romans*, Edinburgh, 5th ed., 1902, pp. 139 and 143.

'The law took its subordinate place.'[3] It is certainly true that in Galatians 2.4, its only other occurrence in the New Testament, παρεισέρχεσθαι does seem to have a somewhat disparaging sense – something like 'insinuate oneself in' or 'intrude'. But Otfried Hofius in his very careful and detailed study of Romans 5.12–21[4] has come out decisively in favour of taking the word here in a neutral sense, 'noch ausserdem hinzukommen'.[5] He argues that, while παρεισέρχεσθαι does sometimes denote a coming in privily, a getting in unnoticed, a getting in by deceit, it is also used in a neutral sense of coming in, entering in addition, coming in besides. He cites a convincing number of clear instances of this neutral use.

But, before we accept his conclusion, it is interesting to look at other Greek words compounded with παρεισ – LSJ lists more than twenty-five – to see whether such a survey confirms Hofius' judgment with regard to παρεισῆλθεν. Four of these words occur in the New Testament: παρεισάγειν in 2 Peter 2.1; παρείσακτος in Galatians 2.4; παρεισδύ(ν)ω in Jude 4; and παρεισφέρειν in 2 Peter 1.5. In the first three of these passages the word in question probably does carry some sense of secrecy (the RV has 'shall privily bring in', 'privily brought in', and 'crept in privily', respectively); but in the last of these passages παρεισφέρειν is clearly quite neutral (σπουδὴν πᾶσαν παρεισενέγκαντες ἐπιχορηγήσατε ἐν τῇ πίστει ὑμῶν τὴν ἀρετήν). In the LXX there is only one occurrence of a παρεισ-compound. It is in 2 Maccabees 8.1, where, though the entering in referred to is certainly secret, the fact that λεληθότως is used with παρεισπορευόμενοι suggests that the verb is understood to mean simply 'make one's way into'. I think it is fair to say that, while a few of the παρεισ–compounds are intrinsically negative in meaning (e.g. παρεισγραφή, in which the addition of παρα-to εἰσγραφή = 'registration' gives the sense 'illegal registration';

[3] Op. cit., pp. 102, 109–10.

[4] 'Die Adam-Christus-Antithese und das Gesetz: Erwägungen zu Röm 5,12–21', in J. D. G. Dunn (ed.), *Paul and the Mosaic Law*, Tübingen, 1996, pp. 165–206.

[5] Op. cit., p. 200.

παρεισπράσσειν, in which the addition of παρα-to εἰσπράσσειν = 'exact' gives the sense 'exact beyond what is legal'; and παρεισφθείρεσθαι, where the simple verb already has a negative meaning), the majority are in themselves quite neutral. Thus, for example, παρεισάγειν can be used equally well of introducing the children of those who have died in war into the assembly (Isocrates 8.82), of proposing someone as a candidate (Plutarch, *Galba* 21), or of traitors treacherously introducing soldiers into a city so as to enable them to take possession of it (Diodorus Siculus, 12.41.4). In Josephus, *BJ* 2.169, παρεισκομίζειν is used of Pilate's introducing into Jerusalem the effigies of Caesar by night and under cover, but it is the identity of what is introduced, the fact that it is concealed and the fact that the action takes place by night, which make this particular παρεισκομίζειν sinister; the verb itself is quite neutral. The situation with regard to παρεισδύ(ν)ω (often in middle voice) meaning 'slip in', 'penetrate' is similar: it can be used of soldiers infiltrating a city (Herodian 2.12), but also of rubbed in oil penetrating into a body (Aristotle, *Problemata* 881ᵃ7) or of water penetrating into a body (ibid., 933ᵃl6), while the cognate παρείσδυσις is used of a slipping in, a way to get in, an opening. My clear impression is that the evidence of the other παρεισ-compounds confirms the conclusion reached by Hofius with regard to παρεισέρχεσθαι, and I think we can be confident that Paul's use of παρεισῆλθεν in Romans 5.20 is in itself in no way a disparagement of the law.

But Hofius, while firmly rejecting the view that παρεισῆλθεν is disparaging, holds that 5.20a sets the law on the Adam-side, not the Christ-side, of the Christ–Adam contrast.[6] Though it does seem probable that, in stating that νόμος . . . παρεισῆλθεν, Paul had in mind his earlier statement in v. 12 that ἡ ἁμαρτία εἰς τὸν κόσμον εἰσῆλθεν καὶ διὰ τῆς ἁμαρτίας ὁ θάνατος, and that by παρεισῆλθεν he meant 'came in [i.e. into the world] besides [i.e. after and in addition to sin and death]', I cannot – for reasons which will presently become clear – accept that this passage places the law on the Adam-side.

---

[6] Op. cit., p. 201.

2. We must next look at ἵνα. John Chrysostom understood it as ecbatic; but it is surely more natural to take it as final. Whose purpose then does Paul have in mind? He does not personify the law in the way he seems sometimes to personify sin. So there can hardly be any thought of the law's deciding to come in besides or of the law's having a purpose in mind. Paul is thinking of God's giving the law (compare the passive προσετέθη in Galatians 3.19), and the purpose indicated by the ἵνα-clause must be God's, as Barrett rightly assumes.[7] The question then arises: Is the final sense strictly limited to the second clause of v. 20a or do vv. 20b-21 also in some way come within its scope? Hofius is emphatic that the final sense is sharply cut off at the end of v. 20a ('Ein finaler Zusammenhang zwischen dem durch die Tora veranlassten "Grosswerden" der Sünde (v. 20a) und dem Auf-den-Plan-Treten der übermächtigen Gnade (v. 20b) wird dabei *nicht* behauptet.')[8] and also that the ἵνα of v. 21 is dependent solely on ὑπερεπερίσσευσεν ἡ χάρις. But Hofius is, I think, putting too much weight on a strict interpretation of the grammar. For, if Paul thought that the last four words of v. 20a expressed a purpose of God in giving the law, must he not also have thought that God would have known both that this purpose would be fulfilled and also that he would respond to this increasing of sin by the superabounding of his grace? And must he not also have thought that God would have seen beyond this superabounding of grace to that ultimate purpose that is expressed in v. 21? It seems to me that, if we recognize that the ἵνα-clause of v. 20 refers to a purpose of God in giving the law, we can hardly avoid understanding that purpose as including both the ὑπερπερισσεύειν of grace to which v. 20 refers and also what is introduced by the ἵνα of v. 21.

3. We must now look more closely at the content of the ἵνα – clause of v. 20a. If what has just been said is on the right lines, we must understand this clause as stating not God's whole purpose in giving the law but an intermediate divine purpose. If sin, already everywhere present and disastrously active in humankind, was

[7] Op. cit., p. 110.
[8] Op. cit., pp. 203, 204.

'ever to be decisively defeated and sinners forgiven in a way worthy of the goodness and mercy of God and recreated in newness of life, it was first of all necessary that sin should increase somewhere among men in the sense of becoming clearly manifest'.[9] I take it that Paul means that God gave the law in order that sin might be recognized in its true character, that is, that sin (here referred to as 'the misdeed' or 'trespass' (τὸ παράπτωμα) might increase[10] in the sense of being recognized as disobedience against God, transgression of his known commandments (παράβασις: compare v. 14, also 4.15b), and human beings' continuing to sin might become the more serious, being now conscious and wilful disobedience. It is possible, indeed likely, that Paul, in using πλεονάσῃ, had in mind also the fact that sin would actually increase in quantity as a result of the coming of the law, since human beings' self-centredness, the illusion that one is God or can become God, which is the essence of sin, is liable to respond with fury and with feverish activity to the attack upon it which God's law represents.[11] It is interesting to compare the way in which the tenants in the parable of Mark 12.1–11 respond to the succession of messengers sent to them by the owner of the vineyard. The more clearly the injustice of their refusal to pay their dues is brought home to them, the more ferocious becomes their treatment of the messengers and their determination to defend their position.

But ἵνα πλεονάσῃ τὸ παράπτωμα is only rightly understood, when it is recognized as a purpose of God, an intermediate purpose which has to be fulfilled, if the ultimate purpose indicated by v. 21 is to be accomplished. Such a full disclosure of the real nature of sin was necessary, if God's redemption of humankind was to be worthy of himself, of his goodness and his faithful love, and therefore free from all condoning or glossing over of evil.

---

[9] My *A Critical and Exegetical Commentary on the Epistle to the Romans* 1, Edinburgh, [7]1990, pp. 292–3.

[10] πλεονάσῃ could here be transitive with τὸ παράπτωμα as its object; but, in view of the fact that in the next clause the same verb must be intransitive, it is more probably intransitive.

[11] Cf. τὰ παθήματα τῶν ἁμαρτιῶν τὰ διὰ τοῦ νόμου in 7.5, also 7.7-11, 13.

But, if this interpretation of v. 20a is on the right lines, how can it possibly be sensible to speak of Romans 5.20, as James Dunn does, in such terms as these: 'Most incriminating of all, "the law came in to increase the trespass" . . .';[12] 'the shocking assertion of 5.20';[13] 'the charge Paul himself brought against the law in 5.20';[14] 'to denigrate the law as he did in 5.20';[15] 'the charge of 5.20'?[16] The truth is, surely, that in this verse Paul is in no way intending to criticize the law. He is indicating one vitally important function which it has in the working out of God's gracious purpose of salvation.

4. οὗ δὲ ἐπλεόνασεν ἡ ἁμαρτία must surely refer to Israel, the people to whom the law was given. In Israel sin was manifest, known as what it is, deliberate disobedience against the one true God. So in this people sin indeed increased, and was exceeding sinful. Nowhere else (except later in the Christian church) could it ever be so serious, since nowhere else would it be such a conscious, deliberate flouting of God's known commandments, such a holding in contempt of his known mercy and generosity. But Paul must surely have had specially in mind the fearful climax of sin's increasing, when the leaders of Israel rejected God's Messiah and handed him over to the Roman authorities to be crucified, and when the Gentile world, represented by Pontius Pilate, responded to the Jewish leaders' pressure and implicit threat to his position by sacrificing justice to expediency. There the sin of humankind, of Jew and Gentile together, reached its climax in the rejection and crucifying of Jesus.

5. It was there that ὑπερεπερίσσευσεν ἡ χάρις in mercy for Israel and for all other peoples. Paul's use of the rare word ὑπερπερισσεύειν (LSJ cites only this passage and 2 Corinthians 7.4: compare also the use of the adverb ὑπερπερισσῶς in Mark 7.37 and of the adverb ὑπερεκπερισσοῦ in Ephesians 3.20;

[12] 'In Search of Common Ground', in *Paul and the Mosaic Law* (see n. 4), p. 322.
[13] Ibid.
[14] Op. cit., p. 323.
[15] Op. cit., p. 324.
[16] Op. cit., p. 331.

1 Thessalonians 3.10; 5.13) marks the climax of the series πολλῷ μᾶλλον and ἐπερίσσευσεν in v. 15, πολλῷ μᾶλλον and περισσείαν in v. 17, πλεονάσῃ and ἐπλεόνασεν in this verse, which is such a prominent feature of this section. That the reference of ὑπερεπερίσσευσεν ἡ χάρις is to God's act in the death and raising up of Jesus is obvious (compare, for example, 5.8; 8.32). It was this act that was the decisive victory of grace.

6. But Paul looks beyond this decisive victory. Verse 21 with its initial ἵνα looks to the goal towards which the superabounding of grace was aimed, the replacement of the reign of sin by the reign of grace. Once more Paul draws a comparison: ὥσπερ ἐβασίλευσεν ἡ ἁμαρτία . . . , οὕτως καὶ ἡ χάρις βασιλεύσῃ . . . And once again it is a comparison between things which in almost all respects are utterly dissimilar. But in one respect they are alike: both sin and grace may be said to reign over those upon whom they have laid hold. Sin's reign results in, and is accompanied by, death, its inescapable concomitant. So closely do they belong together, that in v. 14 Paul was able to say that death reigned. Whereas the character of sin's reign is indicated by the one phrase ἐν τῷ θανάτῳ, Paul sets down three distinct phrases to characterize the reign of grace. Grace, God's grace, established its reign over human beings by conferring upon them the gift of a righteous status before God (for the sense of δικαιοσύνη here compare vv. 16, 17, 18 and 19). That is the significance of the first phrase. The second (εἰς ζωὴν αἰώνιον) indicates the final goal towards which grace brings those over whom it exercises its reign. The third (διὰ Ἰησοῦ Χριστοῦ τοῦ κυρίου ἡμῶν) is fundamental: it is Jesus Christ who establishes and sustains the reign of grace and who is its source. For Paul the grace of God is the grace of Jesus Christ.

In conclusion a number of points must be made.

(i) The ἵνα πλεονάσῃ τὸ παράπτωμα of v. 20a expresses an important, though of course not the only, purpose of God in giving the law.

(ii) Though ὑπερεπερίσσευσεν ἡ χάρις in v. 20b is in no way grammatically a part of what is introduced by the ἵνα of v. 20a and though v. 21 is dependent only on ὑπερεπερίσσευσεν ἡ χάρις, vv. 20 and 21 are nevertheless to be taken closely together, and vv. 20b–21 is to be understood as explicatory of v. 20a.

(iii) By πλεονάσῃ in v. 20a Paul means (a) 'increase' in the sense of becoming manifest, defined, known, recognized; (b) 'increase' in the sense of being enhanced, made more serious (the law by showing human beings that what they are doing is contrary to God's will gives to their continuing to do it the character of conscious and deliberate disobedience); and (c) 'increase' in the sense of increasing in quantity (the law by challenging human beings' self-centredness provokes it to more frantic activity in self-defence).

(iv) The law's making sin to increase in the senses indicated above is a necessary part of God's merciful purpose for the salvation of human beings and for the restoration of his whole creation. Sin had to be revealed in its true character, if God was to forgive and renew human beings in a way worthy of himself as the good, merciful and faithful God he is and consonant with their true dignity as persons morally accountable. What was at stake was surely nothing less than God's being the God he is, and grace's being true, not bogus, grace.

(v) The law, in its action of making sin clearly visible and sharply defined as what it is, belongs (*pace* Hofius) not to the Adam-side but to the Christ-side of the Adam–Christ antithesis. It is not a part of the disease but a necessary part of the cure.

(vi) Romans 5.20 is not at all a criticism of the law.

3

Romans 6.1–14 Revisited

In volume 1 of my commentary on Romans, which was first published in 1975,[1] I suggested that the key to understanding Romans 6.1–14 was to recognize that, for Paul, there are four different senses in which we may speak of our dying with Christ and (corresponding to them) four different senses in which we may speak of our being raised with him, and that these need to be carefully distinguished but at the same time understood in close relation to one another. I still hold by what I then said; but, in view of the importance of this passage in Paul's theology, I want, if I can, to clarify what I was trying to say but failed to make as clear as at the time I thought I had done. I called the four senses: (i) the juridical sense (I regarded 'juridical' as an unsatisfactory description, but could not think of a more suitable single word); (ii) the baptismal sense; (iii) the moral sense; (iv) the eschatological sense. Since in each case we have to do with both (a) a dying with Christ (it is also a dying to sin) and also (b) a being raised with him, we get an eightfold scheme. That Paul has not in these verses expressly set out this eightfold scheme as such is, of course, obvious. My contention was, and is, that what he has said presupposes it, and can be fully understood only if it is borne in mind. My intention is not to undertake here a fresh exegesis of the passage, following the order of Paul's sentences, but rather to look at the elements of this

* First published in *The Expository Times* 106 (1994–95), pp. 40–3.

[1] *A Critical and Exegetical Commentary on the Epistle to the Romans* 1, Edinburgh, [1]1975, pp. 296–320.

eightfold scheme in turn, to see how far all of them can be shown to be present in it either explicitly or implicitly.

(i.a) The first sense, in which, according to Paul as I understand him, we may speak of our dying with Christ is certainly highly paradoxical: we died with Christ on the first Good Friday. This is surely the significance of the preposition 'for' (ὑπέρ) in such places as Romans 5.6 ('Christ died for the ungodly'), 8 ('God commendeth his own love toward us, in that, while we were yet sinners, Christ died for us'); 8.32 ('He that spared not his own Son, but delivered him up for us all'); 14.15 ('him for whom Christ died'); 2 Corinthians 5.14 ('one died for all'), 15 ('he died for all . . . him who for their sakes [Greek: 'for them] died'), 21 ('Him who knew no sin he made to be sin on our behalf' [Greek: 'for us']); Galatians 2.20 ('the Son of God, who . . . gave himself up for me'); 1 Thessalonians 5.10 ('who died for us').[2] God's decision to take our sin upon himself in the person of his own dear Son involved the decision to see Christ's death as died 'for us' and to see us as having died in his death. So this having died with Christ of ours is a matter of God's gracious decision about us. As far as our status with him is concerned, he has chosen to relegate our sinful life to the past. I take it that it is in this sense that Paul refers to himself and the Roman Christians in v. 2 as 'We who died to sin' and in v. 8 argues from the fact of our having died with Christ.[3] This interpretation receives strong support from 2 Corinthians 5.14 ('For the love of Christ constraineth us; because we thus judge, that one died for all, therefore all died'). It is, I think, this death in God's sight to which Romans 7.4 ('Wherefore, my brethren, ye also were made dead to the law through the body of Christ') also refers: compare too v. 6 ('having died to that wherein we were holden'). And Colossians 3.3 ('For ye died') should, of course, also be compared, even though the Pauline authorship of Colossians is disputed.

[2] Cf. Romans 4.25; 1 Corinthians 15.3; Galatians 1.4: in these a 'for us' is implicit.

[3] Though the possibility that Paul was already thinking of baptism in v. 2 and that he may have had it in mind in v. 8 perhaps cannot be altogether excluded, it does not seem very likely.

(i.b) Romans 6.1–14 clearly does not say expressly that Paul and the Roman Christians were raised with Christ on the first Easter morning in God's sight; but vv. 11 and 13 seem to point strongly in this direction. I take it that in the former verse Paul is exhorting the Roman Christians to recognize the truth that they themselves are 'dead unto sin, but alive unto God in Christ Jesus'. That is the truth of the gospel about them. God wills to see them as having died in Christ's death and having been raised in his resurrection. In the latter verse the words 'as alive from the dead' underline the fact that it is a resurrection that is in mind and make it abundantly clear that Paul does think that the people he is addressing have already been raised from the dead in some sense. In view of these two verses, I cannot accept the contention (though it is quite often stated very confidently) that there is a substantial disagreement between this passage and Colossians 3.1, which uses a past tense of the resurrection of believers ('If then [the "if" must here be equivalent to "seeing that"] ye were raised together with Christ'). The facts that in Romans 6 Paul nowhere actually uses a past tense with reference to it and that he uses the future in vv. 5 and 8 ('we shall be also *by the likeness* of his resurrection' and 'we shall also live with him') may indeed reflect his awareness of the danger of misunderstanding on the part of some Christians who are attracted by a false realized eschatology with its illusions of already being filled, already having become rich, already reigning (1 Cor. 4.8). It was – and still is – important to avoid giving any encouragement to such triumphalism. But that Paul, at the time of the writing of Romans, did not think that there is any sense in which believers have already been raised with Christ seems to me to be disproved by these two verses.

(ii.a) The second sense in which we may be said to die with Christ is the baptismal. Verses 3 and 4a indicate that the Roman Christians' baptism is intimately connected with their relationship to Christ's death. They were baptized into his death; through their baptism they were buried with him into death. But, since there are a number of passages in Paul's letters which speak of Christians' death with Christ and new life in him as based on the gospel events themselves and make no mention of baptism (e.g.

Rom. 7.4, 6; 2 Cor. 5.14f, 17; Gal. 2.19f), it is clear that he did not think of baptism as actually effecting this death with Christ. Baptism does not establish the relationship. It attests a relationship already established. For Paul, baptism, which, as the act of the person baptized, is the outward ratification of the human decision of faith,[4] is, as God's act, the sign and seal and pledge that the benefits of Christ's death for all men really do apply to this individual human being in particular. Our baptism is God's confirmation, God's guarantee, of the fact that Christ's death was for us, that God sees us as having died in his death.

(ii.b) Nowhere in Romans 6.1–14 is it said explicitly that those whom Paul is addressing have been raised with Christ in baptism; but it is surely implied. Paul has spoken of their having been baptized into Christ's death; but, if baptism were only the seal of their interest in his death and not also the seal of their interest in his resurrection, it would be of but little value, for Christ's death has no saving efficacy apart from its sequel in his resurrection. There can be no doubt that Paul thought that to be baptized into Christ was to be baptized into him who was not only crucified for us but was also raised up for us. The thought that Christians have been raised with Christ in baptism is surely implicit here. It is possible that its not being made explicit reflects Paul's awareness of the danger of Christian triumphalism (cf. (i.b) above). It is to be noted that Colossians 2.12, by contrast, does speak explicitly of believers as having been raised with Christ in baptism.

(iii.a) Again, it is not expressly said in this passage that Christians have to seek to die daily and hourly to sin – the third sense of our dying with Christ. But it is clearly implied. Thus the response called for by the question, 'We who died to sin, how shall we any longer live therein?' in v. 2 is a recognition that, instead of continuing to live in sin, we must try to die to it. And the thought that we have to strive constantly to die to sin is surely implicit in the last clause of v. 6 ('that we should no longer be in bondage to

---

[4] Where this action of the person baptized is involved, as must usually have been the case in the early days of the church, this element of the rite may be regarded as the beginning of dying and being raised with Christ in sense iii.

sin'), in view of the way in which Paul has expressed himself in the earlier part of the verse ('knowing this, that our old man was crucified with *him*, that the body of sin might be done away'). And, when in v. 11 Paul exhorts the Roman Christians to reckon with the fact that they have already died to sin in God's sight, in God's merciful decision about them, he surely intends them to draw the conclusion that they must now try to die to sin in their actual living. Finally, the same practical conclusion is expressed in different terms in vv. 12 and 13, when he tells them to stop allowing sin to reign unopposed in their mortal selves in such a way that they obey the self's desires and to stop placing their members at sin's disposal as tools of unrighteousness.

Outside this passage the thought of the Christian life as involving a constant striving to die to sin is expressed in various ways. In 8.13 Paul speaks of mortifying (θανατοῦν) the deeds of the body: with this may be compared Colossians 3.5 ('Mortify (νεχϱοῦν) therefore your members which are upon the earth . . .'). The underlying thought is the same, when the image of putting off soiled garments is employed, as in Romans 13.12 ('let us therefore cast off the works of darkness') and Colossians 3.8 ('But now put ye also away all these; anger, wrath, malice . . .').[5] Whether the language used is of divesting oneself of one's clinging sins like a soiled garment or of putting them to death, the basic idea is the same, that the Christian is to try to die daily and hourly to sin. Again, when Paul speaks of the believers' no longer living to themselves (2 Cor. 5.15), the thought of their dying to themselves is close at hand. To die to sin is to reject, renounce, say 'No' to, that idolized self which is the essence of our sinfulness. We may, I think, recognize here a point of contact with Jesus' saying in Mark

---

[5] *Pace* C. F. D. Moule, *The Epistles of Paul the Apostle to the Colossians and to Philemon*, Cambridge, 1957, pp. 117f, and REB, which connect 'out of your mouth' with 'put away', I cannot help thinking that, in view of the presence of the putting off and putting on of clothing metaphor in vv. 9, 10 and 12, and the fact that the same verb is contrasted with 'put on' in Ephesians 4.22 and 24 (and also in Romans 13.12, if the Nestle-Aland text is right), it is more natural to see the putting off of clothing metaphor here than to understand Paul to mean 'banish from your mouths'.

8.34 ('If any man would come after me, let him deny himself'). There is a startlingly memorable sentence in one of John Chrysostom's sermons on Romans, which puts succinctly what we may call the negative side of the imperative of Christian baptism: 'If then thou hast died in baptism, stay dead!' (εἰ τοίνυν ἀπέθανες ἐν τῷ βαπτίσματι, μένε νεκρός).[6] But, as we all learn by experience, the task of staying dead in John Chrysostom's sense is very strenuous, a matter of striving constantly to die afresh to sin.

(iii.b) The truth that Christians must constantly try to allow themselves to be raised with Christ in their day-to-day living is most plainly expressed in v. 4, in which the clause 'as Christ was raised from the dead through the glory of the Father' indicates that the moral conduct denoted by 'walk in newness of life' is being regarded as a resurrection. Coming as it does immediately after v. 4b, which undoubtedly refers to the moral conduct of Christians ('walk' is often used by Paul to denote a person's conduct, as, for example, in 8.4; 13.13; 14.15), v. 5b should also, I think, be understood to refer to Christians' conduct: in our concrete daily living we are to be conformed to Christ's resurrection. The thread of Paul's argument from v. 4b by way of vv. 5b, 6c, 8b through to vv. 12 and 13 seems to me to demand that v. 8b should also be taken to refer to Christians' conduct, though it is possible that the thought of the eschatological fulfilment of the life already begun may also be present. The future indicatives ἐσόμεθα in v. 5b and συζήσομεν in v. 8b are, I suggest, correctly translated 'we are to be' and 'we are to live with'.[7] In v. 11, though 'alive unto God in

[6] J.-P.Migne, *Patrologia Graeca* 60, col. 485.

[7] I suggest that we should recognize here what might be called a future of obligation, 'we are to be', 'we are to live with'. In support of this suggestion the following points may be made: (1) the use of the future indicative to express divine commands is frequently found in the Bible (e.g. the 2nd person singular in the Decalogue and in Deuteronomy 6.5 and Leviticus 19.18; the 2nd person plural in Leviticus 1.2; the 3rd person singular in Leviticus 1.3; the 3rd person plural in Leviticus 1.5): compare the use of the future indicative in English in peremptory commands, as, for example, in the armed forces. (2) We have also the occasional use of the future indicative in the New Testament in deliberative questions (e.g. in Romans 6.1 where 'What shall we say then?' means 'What are

Christ Jesus' is naturally understood as referring to God's gracious decision with regard to the Roman Christians, the imperative 'reckon ye' may be said to denote that intellectual action of recognition and reflection which naturally leads to trying to walk in newness of life. And the duty to allow oneself to be raised with Christ in one's daily living is lastly expressed in the injunction, 'present yourselves unto God, as alive from the dead, and your members *as* instruments of righteousness unto God' (v. 13).

Outside this passage we may recognize the same basic thought, for example, in 2 Corinthians 5.15, where Paul speaks of those who live living 'unto him who for their sakes died and rose again', and in places where the image of putting on fresh clothing is used like Romans 13.12 ('let us put on the armour of light') and 14 ('put ye on the Lord Jesus Christ') and Colossians 3.12 ('Put on therefore . . . a heart of compassion, kindness, humility, meekness, long-suffering').

(iv.a) There is, I think, no reference in Romans 6.1–14 to the fact that we shall finally die to sin, when we actually die. But this is the one item in our eightfold scheme which is unquestionably obvious without being stated. It was doubtless as obvious to Paul as it is to us.

(iv.b) It is possible (as was indicated above) that the thought of our resurrection with Christ in the fourth and last sense (that of our being raised in the final resurrection) is present as a secondary reference in v. 8b (conceivably also in v. 5b) as well as the thought of our resurrection in the moral sense. It is certain that the whole of chapter 6 is enframed by the references to eternal life in 5.21 and 6.22 and 23 – that is, to that eternal life, to which the final

---

we to say then?', and in Luke 22.49, where 'shall we smite with the sword?' means 'are we to smite with the sword?'). The latter example suggests the conceivability of a corresponding 'We shall (not) smite with the sword' in the sense 'We are (not) to smite with the sword'. (3) It would be natural for an officer briefing his company to say to them, 'At such and such an hour we shall do such and such', meaning '. . . we are to . . .' (this being the order he has received). Similarly, in a church service the leader might say, 'After this hymn we shall remain standing . . .', meaning that the intention is that this should happen.

resurrection is the entrance. For explicit statements concerning that final resurrection we have to look outside Romans 6.1–14. Suffice it here to mention just three places out of many which could be cited: Romans 8.11 ('he that raised up Christ Jesus from the dead shall quicken also your mortal bodies through his Spirit that dwelleth in you'); in the same chapter v. 23 ('we ourselves groan within ourselves, waiting for *our* adoption, *to wit*, the redemption of our body'); and, in that passage which is something of a parallel to Romans 6.1–14, Colossians 3.4 ('When Christ, *who is* our life, shall be manifested, then shall ye also with him be manifested in glory').

In conclusion, some loose ends need gathering up. I mentioned above the possibility that Paul's not using past tenses with reference to the resurrection of believers might reflect his awareness of the danger of Christian triumphalism. That he was aware of this danger I regard as certain. But another explanation of what we find particularly in Romans 6.2–5 and 8 is possible, as I suggested in my commentary, namely, that he felt the need to be succinct and so decided to 'appropriate' the dying language to God's merciful decision about us and to our baptism, and to 'appropriate' the resurrection language to the Christian's present life and to the eschatological future, rather than to speak of both dying and being raised in each case. This would make for succinctness. It would give a convenient and tidy arrangement of two and two, and would also have the effect of bringing out the positive nature of the new obedience and of the eschatological future.

The thought of Paul's actually wishing to bring out the positive nature of the Christian's present life may perhaps seem surprising in view of the fact that he had to contend with the sort of illusions to which 1 Corinthians 4.8 refers. But, while I am sure that it is important for us to be on our guard against Christian triumphalism (I for one regard the refusal of some people to recognize the reference of Romans 7.14–25 to Christians as a thoroughly disastrous error!), I think it is equally important that we should not belittle the significance of that newness of life, to which God has certainly called us, however bad we may be at responding to his call. It seems to me that Romans 6.4b, 5b, 8b and

13b should encourage us to recognize that some light from Christ's resurrection falls on even the fumbling and faltering first beginnings of being turned in the direction of obedience which are all we have to show. Those first faint signs of newness of life should not be mistaken for the eschatological glory. The distinction between sense iii and sense iv must certainly not be blurred. But, in our proper determination not so to concentrate on the resurrection as to forget the cross, we must not fail to remember that the fact that Christ himself has already been raised from the dead has a significant bearing on our present life.

4

Sanctification as Freedom: Paul's Teaching on Sanctification

With special reference to the Epistle to the Romans

The bold, categorical statement of Romans 8.2 that 'the law of the Spirit of life has in Christ Jesus set thee free from the law of sin and of death' sums up in a striking way Paul's teaching on sanctification. What he has to say on this subject may, I think, be profitably considered within the framework which this startling affirmation provides.

In the above translation[1] I have assumed that 'in Christ Jesus' is to be connected not with 'life' but with the verb 'has set free', and also that 'thee' is to be accepted as the original reading, the variants, 'me', 'us', and the absence of an expressed object, being readily explicable as assimilation to the use of the first person singular in chapter 7, as assimilation to the first person plural in 8.4, and as an accidental error, respectively. A puzzling feature of the verse is the way in which the word 'law' is used. The right clue to understanding this is, I think, the recognition that Paul is using it metaphorically. He is not referring to the Old Testament law or to any other law in the ordinary sense of the word, but to an authority

---

* First published in *Reformed Review* 48 (1994–95), pp. 217–29 (in issue 3, which was a tribute to Prof. James I. Cook), and republished in *Metanoia* 5 (1995), pp. 194–208.

[1] In this and the other quotations from Romans I have used the translation in my *Romans: a shorter commentary*, Edinburgh, ⁵1995, by permission of T. & T. Clark. The italics in these quotations indicate words without equivalent in the Greek, added in order to complete the sense.

or control that is being exercised. He has already used the word in this metaphorical way more than once in the previous chapter (7.21, 23 (the first and third occurrences of the word), 25 (the second occurrence)). So here by 'the law of the Spirit of life' he means, I take it, the authority, the control, the compelling pressure, which the life–giving Spirit of God exerts upon those whom he indwells, and by 'the law of sin and of death' the authority, control, compelling pressure, exerted by sin, with death as its inevitable consequence. Paul is saying that 'in Christ Jesus', that is, on the basis of what God has done in Christ, the authority exerted by the Holy Spirit has freed the believer from the authority of sin and death.

But, in order to understand this affirmation at all adequately, we must examine it a good deal more closely.

With regard to 'the law of the Spirit of life', it is clear from 8.9 ('But you are not in the flesh but in the Spirit, seeing that God's Spirit dwells in you. (If someone does not possess Christ's Spirit, then he does not belong to Christ.)') that Paul believed that every Christian is indwelt by the Holy Spirit. God has not only come to human beings externally in his Son Jesus Christ and in the message about him; he also comes to them internally, actually entering into them and from within making them open to his external Word, to Jesus Christ. Paul calls the Holy Spirit 'the Spirit of life', that is, the Spirit who gives life; and this description is supported by what is said in 8.6, 10, 11 and 13. Something of what the Spirit's giving of life embraces will become clearer, when the verb 'has set free' is considered. For the moment it is enough to draw attention to the connection with the quotation from Habakkuk 2.4 in 1.17 ('But he who is righteous by faith shall live'). Paul would seem to be pointing to the rôle of the Holy Spirit in the accomplishment of that promise.

By contrast, 'the law of sin and of death' is the power which sin has over us, the bondage in which it holds us, and its inevitable concomitant, the power of death. The essence of sin, according to the Bible, is the attempt to put oneself in God's place, to make one's own ego and the satisfaction of its desires the centre of one's life. That is the fundamental sin of every one of us, whether we are unbelievers or believers. Illuminatingly in Genesis 3 the serpent is represented as setting before Eve the beguiling, flattering, enticing promise, 'ye shall be as God'. Sin is the illusion that one is God, or that one can be God, and all that springs from that illusion. One form which this idolatry of the ego takes – and it is an exceedingly virulent form – is the egotism of the group, whether the family, the tribe, the nation, or the social or economic class (and must we not also reckon with the possibility of a group-egotism of the church?). The law of sin is the dominion exercised over us by this idolatry of the ego. To be enslaved to this law is to be in rebellion against the true God.

In the Greek text, before the verb 'has set free' Paul inserts 'in Christ Jesus'. It is on the basis, and only on the basis, of what God has done in Christ that the liberation, of which he is now speaking, has become possible. Prior to, and basic to, this liberation by the Spirit, which we may call the second liberation, there was a first liberation, that redemption, concerning which 3.21–26 speaks, and to which 4.25; 5.6–9a, 10a also refer. That was the liberation from God's condemnation (8.1) brought about by God's taking upon himself in the person of his own dear Son the guilt, disgrace and grief of all our sin, and dealing with them once for all in his sufferings, his death, his resurrection. It was a liberation altogether objective, accomplished externally to us and altogether independently of us, but on our behalf. It is on the basis of this first liberation accomplished by Christ that the Holy Spirit has now effected that second liberation to which 8.2 refers. The phrase 'in Christ Jesus', then, directs the thoughts of the Roman Christians back to what is the very heart of the gospel, the grace of God in Jesus Christ, as the ultimate source of their release from the law of sin and of death.

There is still one more word which it will be convenient to consider before turning to Paul's 'has set free', and that is the word 'thee'. I have already referred to the fact that there are textual variants here. Their presence is an indication that early copyists were puzzled by the use of the second person singular in this verse. While Paul does quite often elsewhere in Romans, for the sake of greater liveliness, address the individual member as representative of a particular group, using the second person singular, his use of it here is quite unexpected and, moreover, confined to the one word. It is possible to think of several reasons Paul may have had for wanting to make this particular sentence specially striking and emphatic. He may have felt that it was important, in view of the apparent tension between what he was affirming here and what he had just said in the latter part of the previous chapter, to give extra emphasis to his statement, so that there might be no doubt that he was really meaning what he was saying. He may have wanted to bring home to each member of the church the fact that this liberation really did include him or her personally. He may have hoped to challenge each individual to grasp the proffered gift and not be content to be a merely passive object of the Spirit's action.

So we come to the verb 'has set free'. There can scarcely be any doubt that this Greek aorist indicative is affirming that a liberation has actually been accomplished. What then is this liberation? In what sense has the law of the Spirit freed the believer from the law of sin and death? To put the question differently, what does Paul have to tell us, particularly in the Epistle to the Romans, about the Holy Spirit's work of sanctification in the church?

Every serious attempt to answer this question immediately comes up against a difficulty. Clearly Paul's 'has set free' in 8.2 cannot be explained properly in isolation from 7.14–25; and, unfortunately, though, hardly surprisingly, concerning that passage there has been much controversy down the centuries, and its interpretation is still as hotly disputed as ever. The first person singular used in it has been variously explained as referring (i) to Paul's own experience as a Christian; (ii) to his pre-conversion experience as he saw it at the time; (iii) to his pre-conversion experience as seen by him later in the light of his Christian faith; (iv) to the experience of the non-Christian Jew as seen by himself; (v) to the experience of the non-Christian Jew as seen through Christian eyes; (vi) to the experience of the Christian who is still living on an inferior level which could have been left behind; (vii) to the experience of Christians generally. Of these (ii) seems to be ruled out by the verdict which, according to Philippians 3.6b, Paul, before his conversion, passed on his own life. And (iv) may be set aside as being inconsistent with the picture of Jewish self-complacency in chapter 2. The use of present tenses throughout the passage is against both (ii) and (iii), and the order of the sentences in vv. 24–25 is an objection to (ii), (iii), (iv), (v) and (vi); for v. 25b is an embarrassment to all who see in v. 24 the cry of the unconverted person (or of a Christian living on a low level of Christian life) and in v. 25a an indication that the desired deliverance has actually occurred, since, coming after the thanksgiving, it seems to imply that the condition of the speaker after the deliverance is just the same as it was before it. Moreover, v. 24 would be highly melodramatic, if it were not a cry for deliverance from present distress.

Acceptance of (i) or (vii) has seemed impossible to very many, because it has seemed to be incompatible with what Paul has said of the believer's liberation from bondage to sin in 6.6, 14, 17f, 22 and in 8.2 and to involve attributing to him far too gloomy a view of the Christian life. But the other explanations, which take the reference to be to the still unconverted person, are, I am more and more convinced, exegetically unsound and untenable. For the person who speaks in 7.14–25 is one who wills the good and hates the evil (vv. 15, 16, 19, 20), who delights in God's law in his inner man (v. 22) and serves it with his mind (v. 25b). And that is not how Paul depicts the still unconverted. The idea of an internal conflict between a better self and a worse self is, of course, familiar enough to non-Christians; but so serious a conflict as is here described is surely only possible, where the Holy Spirit is present and active. It is the Holy Spirit's work of sanctification which is to be recognized in the willing the good and hating the evil, in the delighting in God's law, in the mind's recognition of, and being engaged to, the law, which are here described. And 'Wretched man that I am! Who will deliver me from this body of death?' (v. 24) is surely far more understandable as the cry of one in whom the Holy Spirit has begun his work and who therefore has begun to have both a true knowledge of sin's tyranny over his life and also a fervent longing for, and a firm hope of, full deliverance from it, than as the cry of one as yet unconverted. For myself I can only conclude that it is (i) or (vii) that should be accepted. As between these two, since the first person singular in vv. 7–13 can hardly be taken as strictly autobiographical, it is probably better to accept (vii) than (i), and to understand Paul to be referring to Christians generally but to recognize that his use of this vivid and forceful way of speaking reflects his deep sense of personal involvement in what he is saying.

If then it is the experience of Christians which is depicted in 7.14–25, it follows that the statement in 8.2 that 'the law of the Spirit of life has . . . set thee free from the law of sin and of death' cannot mean that the Spirit has so fully set the Christian free from the power of sin, that it now has no hold over him. An interpretation of 'has set free' has to be spelled out, which does justice both to the amazing affirmation of 8.2 and also to the confession of 7.14, 'I am carnal, a slave under sin's power'. When it is realized that Paul's doctrine of sanctification is to be found not in chapter 8 in separation from 7.14–25 but in chapters 6–8 taken together (with further working out in 12.1–15.13), and the temptation to oppose 8.1ff (thought of as descriptive of the Christian's situation) to 7.14–25 (thought of as descriptive of the condition of the not yet converted) is resolutely resisted, it becomes possible to reach an understanding of Paul's 'has set free' that is realistic and truly Christian, and that neither encourages in those Christians who are most liable to self-complacency the illusion that they are much better Christians than they actually are, nor robs less self-assured Christians of the encouragement and comfort which they should have from these chapters of Romans.

The following paragraphs are an attempt to draw out the meaning of Paul's 'has set free' and, in so doing, to sketch a rough outline of his teaching on sanctification as set out in Romans.

1. First of all it must be said that this 'has set free' refers to the beginning of an action, not to its completion. What was called above the 'first liberation', that effected by Christ in his death and resurrection, is indeed complete, his finished work; but the liberation which the Spirit works has not been completed for any one, so long as that person's earthly life lasts. The completion of our liberation from the power of sin and of death is not until our death and resurrection. But the beginning of this action is something altogether significant and decisive. When the beginning

has been made, the earnest of final fulfilment is already present. Paul is affirming that the Roman Christians are people, the bonds of whose enslavement to sin, to the tyranny of self, God's Spirit has begun to loosen.

2. The beginning of liberation is the making of a person open to Jesus Christ, the creation of incipient faith. The Holy Spirit frees the human person to begin to believe. Relevant here is 5.5, in which the statement that 'God's love has been poured out in our hearts through the Holy Spirit who has been given to us' is best explained as a pregnant construction, the meaning being that God has lavished his love upon us and its reality has been brought home to our hearts by the Holy Spirit who has been given to us. By bringing home to a person the reality of God's love he creates the response of faith. And the faith he has created he also sustains, increases, renews.

3. Even the first beginnings of faith bring with them a commencement of the renewal of the mind to which 12.2 refers. Paul gives no encouragement at all to anti-intellectualism, to the disparagement of reason. But he recognizes that the intellect is fallen like the rest of the human being. He knows that human beings 'have become futile in their reasonings, and their uncomprehending heart has been darkened' (1.21). Because they have failed to take God into account and have given, each to his own ego, the worship which was due to him alone, their thinking has become disjoined from reality and subject to distortion and corruption. Their fallen minds are flawed and unable to function with proper objectivity. So Paul sees the need for them to be renewed. The renewing of the mind is an essential part of the liberation of which 8.2 speaks, an essential part of the Holy Spirit's work of sanctification. Paul's 'has set free' includes, then, at least a beginning of this renewing of the mind. The power of the Holy Spirit has begun the work of freeing these Christians' minds from the corruption, the distortions, the confusion and the lack of proper objectivity, resulting from their enslavement to self, and bringing their thinking under the discipline of the gospel.

4. The liberation of which Paul speaks is a setting free to resist sin's reign over one's life. When he says to the Roman Christians

'Stop, then, allowing sin to reign *unopposed* in your mortal selves
. . . stop placing your members at the disposal of sin . . .' (6.12–
13), he is bidding them do something they could not do, had not
the Holy Spirit made them free to do it. It is the Holy Spirit who
sets us free to stop permitting sin's tyranny over us to go unchallenged, to stop yielding up all our capacities tamely for sin to
exploit, to begin to rebel against the usurper and to fight back in
support of our rightful owner, God. We have not been freed in the
sense that sin has no longer any hold on us; but we have been freed
to the extent that we need no longer be sin's unresisting slaves.
The Christian is like a country which, having been overrun and
occupied by a brutal enemy, is at last being invaded by a friendly
force determined to drive out the occupying power. As the inhabitants of an occupied country might rise up against the occupying
power, so the Christian is now in a position at least to show on
whose side his sympathies are by putting up some resistance to the
tyranny of his own ego, the reign of sin over his life. In the conflict
which is being waged between the Holy Spirit and the occupying
power of sin he may now begin to act as the Holy Spirit's partisan,
one who seeks to walk 'not . . . according to the flesh but according
to the Spirit' (8.4).

5. The Spirit who has freed us to begin to resist sin's tyranny
over us is also 'the Spirit of adoption by whose enabling we cry,
"Abba, Father"' (8.15). He has made us free to address God by
the name of 'Father', assuring us 'that we are children of God'
(8.16). Paul uses in v. 15 the present indicative, 'we cry'. If we are
Christians at all, we do this, though it may be only very feebly,
very falteringly, and with very limited comprehension of what we
are doing. It is the Holy Spirit's continuing work of sanctification
to make us do it more and more understandingly, sincerely,
confidently, humbly. And to address God as Father sincerely and
seriously must mean trying to live as his children and therefore
striving with all one's might to be and think and say and do what
is well-pleasing to him and to avoid all that displeases him. One
implication of this addressing God as Father, which down the
centuries Christians have been strangely slow to recognize, may be
mentioned here, namely, that thus to address God the Creator

carries with it the obligation to respect the creation as his creation and to refrain from all abuse of it. And this must surely include treating with considerateness and compassion all those creatures he has endowed with the capacity to feel pain and fear, and respecting the dignity which inalienably belongs to them as his sentient creatures. In this connection 8.19–22 is surely highly significant both by reason of its contents and also by reason of its being placed where it is in chapter 8.

6. In enabling us to cry 'Abba, Father' the Holy Spirit makes us free to engage in Christian prayer. The gift of the freedom to pray and the sustaining of that freedom from day to day are a vital part of our sanctification. The 'has set free' of 8.2 means that those who are being addressed have at least been so far liberated from the tyranny of their self-centredness that prayer is now a real possibility for them. The loneliness and isolation of their slavery to sin have begun to be overcome. Instead of being altogether turned in on themselves they are free to turn towards God, to enter into conversation with him, and more and more to live consciously in his presence. Paul recognizes that the believer's praying is characterized by weakness and ignorance, and is altogether dependent on the Holy Spirit's help. Thus he writes in 8.26–27: 'the Spirit also helps our weakness; for we do not know what it is right for us to pray for, but the Spirit himself intercedes for us with unspoken groanings, and he who searches the hearts knows what is the intention of the Spirit, that he is interceding for the saints according to God's will'. At the same time, he knows that the freedom, which the Spirit gives, is real freedom and that the believers in Rome have therefore a serious part to play. So he writes to them: 'I exhort you [, brethren,] by our Lord Jesus Christ and by the love of the Spirit to join earnestly with me in prayers on my behalf to God, that I may be delivered from the disobedient in Judaea and that my ministry to Jerusalem may be acceptable to the saints, so that, if it be God's will, my coming to you may be a matter of joy and I may find full refreshment in your fellowship' (15.30–31). Paul's use of συναγωνίσασθαι (which we have rendered by 'join earnestly with') at least suggests that he sees the believer's part in prayer as a serious, indeed, a strenuous activity. Elsewhere he bids

them 'persevere in prayer' (12.12). He realizes how strong the temptation will be to give up praying or at least to become careless and slack about it. It is, I think, clear that, for Paul, it is vitally important that Christians should use to the full that freedom to pray which the Holy Spirit has given them, persisting steadfastly both in prayers together in the Christian community and in private prayers, and also trying at all times to live prayerfully.

7. The liberation of which 8.2 speaks is also a setting free to turn in the direction of obedience to God's law, to make a beginning of trying seriously to obey it. I think it is fair to say that to address, and continue addressing, the true God as Father (8.15b) with full understanding, full seriousness, full sincerity, is all that God's law requires of us. But, since our praying 'Abba, Father' is not yet with such fullness of understanding, seriousness and sincerity, we cannot dispense with the help and guidance which God's law affords. Despite opinions to the contrary often expressed, I am still convinced that Paul regards the Old Testament law as having continuing validity for Christians, though recognizing – and this is extremely important – that, because its true meaning has now been made manifest in Jesus Christ, the relation of Christians to it is fundamentally different from the relation to it of those who do not yet believe in him.[2] They will no longer imagine that it is something which they can so adequately fulfil as to establish a claim on God. Nor will they any more understand it in isolation from him, who is its 'goal' (so I understand *telos* in 10.4). But they will understand it, as it is illuminated and clarified by the life, death, resurrection and exaltation of Jesus Christ, as being both witness to him and his saving work and also a God-given guide for their attempts to live as God's children. It is, I think, implied by 8.3–4 taken in conjunction with 8.2 that the liberation which the Holy Spirit effects must include a beginning in the lives of Christians of that fulfilment of the law which God intended to bring about when he sent his

---

[2] Reference may be made to my article, 'Has the Old Testament law a place in the Christian life? A response to Professor Westerholm', in *Irish Biblical Studies* 15 (1993), pp. 50–64, reprinted below as Chapter 9.

Son to deal with sin. Significantly Paul uses in 8.4 the singular τὸ δικαίωμα ('the righteous requirement'), bringing out the essential and intelligible unity behind and beneath the multiplicity of the law's commands. In 7.14–25 we have a vivid picture of the conflict which takes place in those in whom the Holy Spirit is carrying on his work of sanctification. Here is one who has been freed to will the good and to hate the evil (vv. 15, 16, 19, 20), who already in his 'inner man' (that is, that new self which the Holy Spirit has brought into being) 'delight[s] in God's law' (v. 22) and with his 'mind' (that is, his mind as it is being renewed by the Holy Spirit (cf. 12.2)) 'serve[s] the law of God' (v. 25b). Here is one who in the depths of his personality in so far as it has been renewed is engaged to God's law. In this person the promise of Jeremiah 31.33 has begun to be fulfilled: 'I will put my law in their inward parts, and in their heart will I write it.'

8. But the Old Testament law itself provides a summary of what its righteous requirement means in the two passages (Deut. 6.4–5; Lev. 19.18b) which Jesus quoted in answer to the scribe's question (Mark 12.28–34; Matt. 22.34–40). What the law requires is that one should love God with all one's heart and soul and might and should love one's neighbour as oneself. So the freedom to try to obey God's law, which the Holy Spirit has given to us, is freedom to try to love God with all one's heart and soul and might and to love one's neighbour as oneself. Since ἡ ἀγάπη τοῦ θεοῦ in 5.5 surely refers to God's love for us, not our love to God, there is only one place in Romans where ἀγάπη or ἀγαπᾶν is used with reference to human beings' love to God, and that is 8.28: 'And we know that all things prove advantageous for *their true* good to those who love God'. But this is evidence enough that Paul thinks of believers as people who love God. The liberation, of which 8.2 speaks, is a setting free at least to begin to love God. But Paul speaks more often of the love which Christians owe their fellow human beings. In 12.9 ('Let *your* love be genuine') the reference is probably to love for fellow human beings generally, since the next verse ('In *your* love for the brethren show one another affectionate kindness') will have more point, if the love mentioned in v. 9 is not just the same thing as the love for the brethren referred to in v. 10,

but an all-embracing love. All-embracing too most probably is the love enjoined in 13.8–10, since the universal negative with which v. 8 begins makes it natural to understand 'one another' and 'the other' in v. 8 and 'neighbour' in vv. 9 and 10 in the widest possible sense. But in 14.15 ('For, if thy brother is grieved on account of *thy* food, thou walkest no longer in accordance with love') it is love between Christians that Paul has in mind. In 15.30, where the phrase 'the love of the Spirit' means 'the love which the Spirit works', the context suggests it is love between Christians that is specially in mind; but the expression is witness to Paul's belief that it is the Holy Spirit who makes Christians free to love their fellow human beings. One further point may be made here, namely, that it ought to be recognized as highly significant that 13.1–7 has been placed between 12.9–21 and 13.8–10, two passages concerned with love. Was not Calvin right in saying that the fulfilment of what is enjoined in 13.1–7 'constitutes not the least part of love'?[3] Must we not recognize that trying seriously to fulfil our political responsibility as Christians, which in a democracy is a very onerous matter, is an important part of the love of the neighbour for which the Holy Spirit sets us free, an important part of our sanctification?

9. But consideration of the thrice repeated 'all' of Deuteronomy 6.5, a commandment Paul surely knows and accepts, though in 13.9 he omits to quote it, because he is there concerned with love to the neighbour; of the indication in 13.8 that the debt of love is never fully discharged; of the 'as thyself' in 13.9 which makes it clear that the love for the neighbour required of us is a love no whit less real and sincere than the love which all of us sinners have for ourselves; of the searching exhortations of 12.9–21, a section which might be entitled 'marks of love'; and of what is said in 14.1–15.13 of the sensitiveness and gentleness, which should characterize relations within the church, must surely lead us to recognize how far short we fall of the love God's law requires of us. And, if for a moment we glance outside Romans, the portrait of love which we find in Galatians 5.22–23 (it is surely right to

---

[3] *The Epistles of Paul the Apostle to the Romans and to the Thessalonians*, translated by R. Mackenzie, Edinburgh, 1961, p. 285.

understand the last eight substantives in the list of nine not as separate items but as depicting the characteristics of true love) must powerfully reinforce our conclusion. It would indeed be a mightily self-complacent Christian who could look at this portrait of the love which is joyful, never grudging or sullen; which is marked by peace with God, with fellow human beings and within one's own inner being; which is longsuffering, patient, giving others room and time; which is kind in intention and in action; which is truly good both in the sense of having integrity and in the sense of being generous; which is faithful, not liable to fail or grow weary or betray the hopes placed in it; which is gentle, not self-assertive or aggressive, not determined to love in one's own way even though that way may be damaging to the person one is supposed to be loving; which is self-controlled, truly disciplined in its unselfishness and, having looked, could say, 'Yes, this is a true portrait of the love which my life shows'. By freeing us to try seriously to love God and our neighbour, the Holy Spirit makes us free for penitence, so that we may live each day and hour by the forgiveness of sins, learning more and more fully how far short we fall of perfect Christian love. Penitence is a distinguishing mark of all who are being sanctified.

10. The liberation spoken of in 8.2 is the setting free of those who have already died and been raised with Christ in God's sight in that he died and was raised for them, and have already died and been raised with Christ in their baptism as the seal and pledge of God's gracious decision so to see them, now also to die with Christ and be raised with him in their actual living, as they strive again and again to die to sin and to rise to newness of life. In 6.1–14, probably both for the sake of brevity and also in order to bring out the positive nature of the Christian's obedience, Paul speaks (vv. 4 and 5) of our dying and being raised in baptism only in terms of death and of our moral dying to sin and being raised to newness of life only in terms of resurrection ('So then we have been buried together with him through baptism into *his* death, in order that, as Christ was raised from the dead through the glory of the Father, so we also might walk in newness of life. For if we have been conformed to his death, we are certainly also to be *conformed* to his

resurrection.'). In 8.13, however, he does use the language of dying with reference to dying in the moral sense.

11. This setting free to die again and again to sin and to rise again and again to newness of life is a setting free for life which is truly called life because it is turned in the direction of obedience to God. In the believer's walking in newness of life, even though falteringly, the promise of 1.17 that 'he who is righteous by faith shall live' has begun to be fulfilled. But this is only a partial fulfilment. We have yet to die with Christ in our actual death and to be raised with him finally. The life, for which 'the Spirit of life' has set us free, includes both newness of life in this world and also eternal life hereafter. That this is a constant theme of Romans can be seen from 1.17; 2.7; 4.17; 5.17, 18, 21; 6.4, 8, 11, 13, 22, 23; 7.10, 24–25a; 8.2, 6, 10, 11, 13; 11.15; 12.1.

12. Another prominent theme of Romans is hope, the noun ἐλπίς occurring thirteen times (that is, much more frequently than in any other New Testament book) and the verb ἐλπίζειν four times. It is clear that, for Paul, the freedom which the life-giving Spirit imparts is also freedom for hope. The subsection 8.17–30, in particular, is concerned with Christian hope. The movement of thought from sonship to heirship in v. 17 introduces the subject. Verses 18, 19, 21 and the last part of v. 23 give an indication of what is hoped for and of its transcendent worth. They also make it clear that this hope is not just an individual matter, but is hope for God's whole creation. 'I reckon', says Paul, 'that the sufferings of the present time are not worthy to be compared with the glory which is to be revealed in us . . . the creation itself too shall be set free from the bondage of decay into the liberty of the glory of the children of God'; and he specifies as the object of our hope, as that for which we wait, 'the redemption of our bodies'. It is that which will be the full manifestation of the adoption as God's children, which is already ours, though hidden. At the same time the references to 'the sufferings of the present time' (v. 18), to the creation's having been subjected to vanity (v 20), to the groaning and travailing together of the whole creation (v. 22), to the groaning of believers (v. 23), and to the steadfast patience with which they have to wait for what they hope for (v. 25), all point to the

painfulness characteristic of the circumstances in which their hope has now to be exercised. The last three verses of the subsection express its certainty. But the subject of hope was already hinted at in 8.10–11. And as early in the epistle as chapter 4 the Christian's hope is foreshadowed in the hope of Abraham, the type of the believer, firmly hoping in God's promise in defiance of all human expectations (4.18), while in 5.2–5 Paul declares: 'we exult in hope of the glory of God. And not only so, but we even exult in afflictions, knowing that affliction works endurance, and endurance provedness, and provedness hope. And this hope does not put us to shame . . . '. In 13.11–14 no word of the ἐλπίς group is used, but the passage is concerned with the Christian hope. The fact that what the Roman Christians hope for, their final salvation at Christ's coming, draws ever nearer renders all the more urgent their obligation to use the present time for obedience of life. For Paul it is of the utmost importance that Christians should continue to hope. So he tells them that it was in order 'that with patient endurance and *strengthened* by the comfort which the scriptures give we might hold hope fast' (15.4) that the scriptures were written; and he closes the hortatory main division 12.1–15.13 with the prayer-wish, 'May the God of hope fill you with all joy and peace in believing, so that you may abound in hope by the power of the Holy Spirit' (15.13). This last quotation and also 12.12, in which Paul exhorts the Roman Christians to 'rejoice in hope', point forward by their associating hope with joy to the subject of the next paragraph.

13. The freedom which the Holy Spirit effects is freedom to rejoice. With 12.12 and 15.13, just mentioned, the references to exulting (καυχᾶσθαι) in 5.2, 3 and 11 may be compared. In 14.17 Paul defines the kingdom of God, that is, the kingdom of God in its present reality, as 'righteousness and peace and joy in the Holy Spirit'. This joy, which is the Spirit's work in the believer and altogether different from all joys that are merely the temporary results of the satisfaction of one's own selfish desires, is one of the things which attest the kingdom's presence. It is not without significance that in the ninefold list of Galatians 5.22–23 'joy' is placed immediately after 'love'.

14. One thing which has been implicit in what has been said in the foregoing paragraphs about Paul's 'has set free' must now be stated explicitly. It is that the liberation which the Holy Spirit effects is liberation for fellowship with all others whom he has begun to set free, for membership of the company of those who believe in Jesus Christ, the community of his church. Whereas the word for 'church' occurs twenty-two times in 1 Corinthians and nine times in 2 Corinthians, it occurs only five times in Romans, and whereas it is present in the opening verses of 1 and 2 Corinthians, Galatians and 1 Thessalonians, all five of its occurrences in Romans are in chapter 16. But it would be a very big mistake to conclude that the church is relatively unimportant in Romans. In fact, the reality and importance of the church, the company of believers, is everywhere presupposed. Very often Paul's use of the first person plural reflects his consciousness of belonging, along with those he is addressing, to a community of faith. And, when he uses the second person plural, it is generally apparent that he is not addressing the Roman Christians as isolated individuals, but as members together of the church. Paul's hopes and fears with regard to their life as a community and the quality of their relations one with another are vividly reflected in 12.1–15.13, but also elsewhere in the epistle. There can be no doubt that he thinks of the sanctification of believers not as a sanctification of individuals in isolation but as the sanctification of individuals within the fellowship of the church. The liberation of which 8.2 speaks is a setting free to participate gladly and hopefully in the common life of the community of believers, sharing in responsibility for its common obedience to Jesus Christ.

In conclusion four observations may be made.

(i) It is abundantly clear that 8.2, while it is formulated only in terms of *freedom from*, carries also a rich positive *freedom for* significance.

(ii) While the work of sanctification, the freeing of human beings from the power of sin and death, is the work of the Holy Spirit, the many sentences in Romans which convey an imperative (a variety of forms are used – see, for example, 6.13; 13.12b; 12.1; 12.3; 6.12; 15.2) prove conclusively that Paul does not think of the believer's part as being that of a merely passive spectator of the Spirit's work. An active response is called for.

(iii) Paul takes it for granted that every Christian is indwelt by the Holy Spirit (8.9a). If we show in our lives no trace at all of his sanctifying work, that can only mean that we are not yet Christians ('If someone does not possess Christ's Spirit, then he does not belong to Christ' (8.9b)). If the Holy Spirit is really at work in one's life, there will be some evidence at least of penitence, of awareness of one's need of forgiveness, both God's and one's neighbour's.

(iv) While it is important to recognize that the 'has set free' of 8.2 certainly does not mean that the life of the believer is a triumphant progress from victory to victory such as some Christians are prone to imagine, it is also of the utmost importance to recognize that we cannot thank God enough for the fact that in the darkness of this world as we know it the Holy Spirit never ceases to carry on his sanctifying work. And, if God does not despise but actually values the faltering and fumbling beginnings of being turned in the direction of obedience, seen in the lives of Christians, can we ever cease from marvelling at such ineffable grace?

The above very slight contribution to the discussion of a great theme is offered as an expression of deep indebtedness to, and affection for, the distinguished scholar, highly valued teacher, and faithful pastor, in whose honour this essay is published.

5

Some Comments on Professor J. D. G. Dunn's *Christology in the Making*

With special reference to the evidence
of the Epistle to the Romans

The publication of any new book of serious scholarship on the subject of New Testament christology is an important event. When the book is arrestingly written and is capable of provoking to activity even sluggish minds and compelling them to work over afresh questions of the greatest importance, it will be no surprise if it stirs up a considerable flurry of reactions. Such a book is Professor Dunn's *Christology in the Making*.[1] It undoubtedly requires and deserves careful and critical attention. The resolute application and sheer physical stamina of one who can write so substantial a book, requiring so much hard thought and at the same time involving the vast amount of research which the bibliography attests, in so short a time (on p. x Professor Dunn observes that the project 'has filled most of my research time for the past three years') command unbounded admiration. It is an astounding

* First published in L. D. Hurst and N. T. Wright (ed.), *The Glory of Christ in the New Testament: Studies in Christology in Memory of George Bradford Caird*, Oxford, 1987, pp. 267–80 and reprinted by permission of Oxford University Press.

---

[1] J. D. G. Dunn, *Christology in the Making: A New Testament Inquiry into the Origins of the Doctrine of the Incarnation*, London, 1980.

achievement – all the more so, as it is written with a light touch and is free from the reek of small hours' oil, though a great deal of that substance must surely have been expended on it. And it does not stand alone, but is flanked by a number of articles supporting and supplementing it, which Professor Dunn has published in recent years.[2]

To respond at all adequately to so important and already influential a book within the space which I can take is beyond my powers. What I shall attempt to do is first to make some general comments, then to refer to the exegesis of passages from Romans contained in the book, and finally to consider some features of that epistle which seem to me to have been given too little attention in it or to have been ignored.

I

Professor Dunn tells us that he has deliberately refrained from attempting 'to define "incarnation" at the outset' because of 'the considerable risk that any such definition would pre-set the terms and categories of the investigation and prevent the New Testament authors speaking to us in their own terms' (p. 9). Had he been intending to consider all, or, at any rate, as much as possible, of the evidence which could be relevant, this procedure might have been feasible. But, since he was going to be highly selective with regard to the evidence to be considered, the method has (so it seems to me) a serious defect. For, though he does not give his readers a definition of 'incarnation' at the outset, he must of necessity have had a working definition of it in mind, by which to determine what material had to be examined and what might be ignored; and a definition, undeclared to the reader but present all the time in the author's mind controlling his selection of the evidence to be considered, was surely likely to 'pre-set the terms and categories of the investigation and prevent the New Testament authors speaking to us in their own terms' (p. 9) at least as effectively as,

---

[2] E.g. 'Was Christianity a monotheistic faith from the beginning?', in *SJT* 35 (1982), pp. 303–36; 'In defence of a methodology', in *ET* 95 (1983–84), pp. 295–9.

and potentially much more damagingly than, one shared with the reader from the start. So the working definition, by which Professor Dunn selected his evidence, should surely have been declared from the beginning.

Moreover, he was not concerned with a general idea of incarnation, but was conducting '*a historical investigation into how and in what terms the doctrine of the incarnation first came to expression*, an endeavour to understand in its original context the language which initially enshrined the doctrine of the incarnation or out of which the doctrine grew' (p. 10). Presumably the definite articles placed before 'doctrine' and 'incarnation' each time the words occur in this sentence and also in the subtitle of the book are meant to indicate that the reference is quite specifically to the historic Christian doctrine of the Incarnation. But, if that is so, would it not have been wise to state near the beginning briefly but clearly that historic Christian doctrine so as to save the readers from any doubt or confusion as to what precisely it is, the first coming to expression of which the author is seeking to investigate? Certainly the attempt must be made to understand the language used for this expression 'in its original context' (p. 10), to 'let the New Testament evidence speak in its own terms and dictate its own patterns' (p. 9), and to bear constantly in mind the danger of our misunderstanding the original intentions of the earliest Christian writers through reading back into what they have said the thoughts of later times (with none of this is any competent New Testament scholar likely to quarrel). But at the same time we ought to recognize the possibility of our mistaking a vision distorted by reaction against the orthodoxy of later times for an authentic seeing with the eyes of the earliest Christians. That the omission of a brief but clear statement of the sort indicated above has really facilitated an objective understanding of the New Testament evidence in its own historical context seems to us highly unlikely. Is it not more likely that it has resulted in failure to recognize the relevance to the subject of inquiry of some New Testament material, and so has led to the exclusion from consideration of some things which ought to have been considered?

Professor Dunn himself is well aware that the Christian doctrine of the Incarnation cannot be properly understood except in the context of the Christian doctrine of the Trinity. He is also conscious of the fact that an insufficiently informed and thoughtful zeal for maintaining the doctrine of the Incarnation can betray people into tritheism.[3] Yet, while his index of subjects contains a few references under 'Trinitarian tendency', such a prime Pauline passage for the doctrine of the Trinity – and surely also for the doctrine of the Incarnation – as 2 Corinthians 13.13 [RV: 14] does not seem to be mentioned at all in the book. Reading *Christology in the Making* led me to re-read once again that part of Karl Barth's *Church Dogmatics* I/1 which is concerned with the doctrine of the Trinity, and I cannot help wondering whether, had Professor Dunn re-read these pages when he was engaged with his book, he might not have been persuaded of the relevance to his subject of some New Testament material which he has excluded from his discussion and also encouraged to be more precise in his use of language with regard to the pre-existence of Christ than he has been. But there is only one reference to Barth in his index of authors.

II

In the second place, we turn to a consideration of Professor Dunn's exegesis of passages in Romans. There are in all thirteen passages of Romans, of which, according to the index of New Testament references, some exegesis is offered; but we shall here consider only those five of them which bear directly on the question whether or not the doctrine of the Incarnation can be discerned in Paul's Epistle to the Romans.

The first is 1.3–4. On pp. 33–5 Professor Dunn is attempting to draw out the meaning, not of these verses in their present context, but of the pre-Pauline formula which he thinks Paul has incorporated. While I am inclined to agree that the suggestion that Paul is making use of an already existing formula is probable, I do

---

[3] See *ET* 95 (1983–84), p. 299.

not share Professor Dunn's confidence that we can be sure of the sense it carried originally, not knowing its original context. I cannot see how his statement that it is 'clear . . . that *there is no thought of a pre-existent sonship here*' (that is, in the presumed pre-Pauline formula) can be justified. That this thought could have been present is surely not inconceivable, particularly if 'in power' was part of the original formula (an alternative he admits as possible). There are other statements in these pages which seem to me questionable. But, as I am now concerned with the sense of the passage in its context in Romans, I pass on to his suggestion on pp. 138f that 'it is possible that Paul meant [by the 'according to the flesh/according to the Spirit' antithesis] that Jesus' installation as Son of God (in power) "according to the Spirit" was in part at least the consequence of his having lived "according to the Spirit"'.[4] Paul's κατὰ πνεῦμα ἁγιωσύνης is notoriously difficult and has been very variously interpreted. Professor Dunn's explanation seems less probable than that which takes the phrase to refer to the presence of the Holy Spirit, which, as resulting from Christ's exaltation, is the guarantee of his having been appointed Son of God in power since his resurrection. For one thing, an interpretation which understands the times to which the two phrases κατὰ πνεῦμα ἁγιωσύνης and ἐξ ἀναστάσεως νεκρῶν refer, to be the same, is surely preferable to one which assumes a temporal disjunction between them, as does Professor Dunn's. What is most important for our present purpose is that Professor Dunn does not consider anywhere in *Christology in the Making* (as far as I can see) the possibility that κατὰ σάρκα is intended to limit the application of τοῦ γενομένου ἐκ σπέρματος Δαυίδ to the human nature which the One, who has already been described as God's Son at the beginning of v. 3, assumed, or, to put it in other words, that the point of κατὰ σάρκα is, in fact, to indicate that, true though it is – and it is indeed of real importance – that, as far as his manhood is concerned, the Son of God is the legal descendant of David, his manhood is not coextensive with

---

[4] Cf. J. D. G. Dunn, 'Jesus – Flesh and Spirit: an exposition of Romans 1.3–4', in *JTS* n.s. 24 (1973), pp. 40–68.

the fullness of his person. The use of κατὰ σάρκα here may be compared with its use in 9.5. While it is true that, treated as an isolated scrap of evidence, these verses do not afford any incontrovertible proof that the writer believed in the pre-existence of Christ and in his incarnation, understood in their context and in the light of the rest of Romans, they are significant support for the view that he did so.

The second passage is 8.3. Professor Dunn's treatment of this key-verse is scattered over several places (in particular, pp. 44f, 111f and 126f), but there is no really thorough discussion of it. The reference of πέμψας to the sending into the world of the pre-existent Son is not to be dismissed so lightly. It is true that the use of πέμπειν (as also of ἐξαποστέλλειν in Gal. 4.4) does not in itself require such a reference; for the language of 'sending' is often used in the Bible of the divine commissioning of prophets. But the fact that the reference to the divine sending and the description of the One sent as God's Son (note here the specially emphatic τὸν ἑαυτοῦ υἱόν) are followed both here and in Galatians 4.4 by words which are naturally understood as indicating the consequence of the sending for the One sent, namely, that he comes to have a human existence (in Rom. 8.3 the words ἐν ὁμοιώματι σαρκὸς ἁμαρτίας and in Gal. 4.4 the words γενόμενον ἐκ γυναικός, γενόμενον ὑπὸ νόμον), surely makes it very difficult to avoid the conclusion that in both places we are up against strong evidence of the presence of the doctrine of the Incarnation in Paul's thought.[5]

But more must be said about 8.3. An obvious problem is: Why did Paul not just say ἐν σαρκὶ ἁμαρτίας? Why did he insert ἐν ὁμοιώματι and put the genitive σαρκός instead of σαρκί? This has been much discussed and various explanations have been offered. Professor Dunn simply assumes, without consideration of other views, that the meaning of ἐν ὁμοιώματι σαρκὸς ἁμαρτίας is 'in the (precise) likeness of sinful flesh' (pp. 44 and 45) and that Paul wanted to make 'an affirmation of the complete oneness of Christ with sinful man making his death effective for the

---

[5] Reference should be made to E. Schweizer, in *TWNT* 8, pp. 376–8 and 385f.

condemnation of sin by the destruction of its power base (the flesh)' (p. 45). The purpose of Professor Dunn's addition of the word 'precise' is not absolutely clear. Was it perhaps to indicate agreement with the suggestion that ὁμοίωμα here means 'form' rather than 'likeness'? This suggestion can certainly be defended, but its correctness should not be taken for granted. As a matter of fact, much of the attention of interpreters of Romans has been directed towards explaining why Paul should introduce the idea of likeness here. But of this *Christology in the Making* gives no hint. Of the suggestions which might have been discussed the one which still seems to me the most probable is that Paul did it in order to take account of the truth that God's Son was not changed into man, but, while assuming our fallen human nature and becoming truly man, still remained himself. According to this suggestion, the use of ὁμοίωμα was intended to guard against the notion of a 'complete oneness of Christ with sinful man' (p. 45) in the sense of a oneness which is so complete that there is a time when he is fallen man without remainder – not to call in question the reality of his true humanity, the reality of his sharing our fallen human nature, but to draw attention to the fact that in becoming man the Son of God never ceased to be himself.[6] (Here the ἐν ὁμοιώματι ἀνθρώπων γενόμενος of Phil. 2.7 is to be compared.) Professor Dunn does not mention this suggestion, as far as I can see. But to assume that Paul could not conceivably have thought in such a way is surely to underestimate his intelligence.

The third passage is 8.9–11. Professor Dunn has some discussion of these verses on pp. 144–6. He refers to 'the familiar observation that in Romans 8.9–11 "Spirit of God dwells in you", "you have the Spirit of Christ", and "Christ is in you" are all more or less synonymous formulations' (p. 145). But he does not consider the possibility that the parallelism between 'the Spirit of God' and

---

[6] Professor Dunn's 'wholly' in his sentence, 'it was the first Christians' recognition *both* of the reality of God in Christ *and* that Christ was wholly one with them, a man among men, that determined the course of future orthodoxy', in *SJT* 35 (1982), p. 335, is to be questioned. Is there not a vital distinction between *vere* and *totaliter*, which must not be blurred, if we are to keep to Christian truth?

'the Spirit of Christ' in v. 9 is one more evidence of Paul's recognition of the divine dignity, and therefore of the pre-existence, of Christ.

The fourth passage is 9.5. Professor Dunn gives it less than half a page altogether. This is surprisingly slight treatment in view of the fact that he himself admits 'the very real possibility that *Romans 9.5* refers to Christ as God (θεός)' (p. 45). It is also marked by an uncharacteristic looseness, which leaves the reader puzzled, if he tries to analyse what exactly is being said. Was Professor Dunn unhappy with this piece of evidence? One sentence states that 'the punctuation intended by Paul and the meaning of the doxology is [*sic*] too uncertain for us to place any great weight on it'; but the very next sentence is: 'The argument on punctuation certainly favours a reference to Christ as "god".' After the confusing combination of 'too uncertain' and 'certainly', we are told that 'Paul's style is notably irregular and a doxology to Christ as god at this stage would be even more unusual within the context of Paul's thought than an unexpected twist in grammatical construction'. But is Paul's style so 'notably irregular'? And is 'an unexpected twist in grammatical construction' an adequate description of the difficulty involved in taking v. 5b as an independent doxology? Professor Dunn goes on to assert that 'Even if Paul does bless Christ as "god" here, the meaning of "god" remains uncertain, particularly in view of our earlier discussion (above pp. 16f)'; but the material gathered on pp. 16f seems to have very little in common with Romans 9.5. The last sentence of p. 45 ('Whatever the correct rendering of the text it is by no means clear that Paul thinks of Christ here as pre-existent god') would seem to suggest that even in Professor Dunn's own mind there remains sufficient doubt to make imperative a much more serious discussion of the various arguments which have been put forward in connection with this verse than he has given us. It is true that several recent commentators[7] have rejected the reference of v. 5b to Christ; but it is significant that they had not had the chance to consider the extremely careful contribution by B. M. Metzger entitled 'The

[7] E.g. E. Käsemann, O. Kuss, U. Wilckens.

Punctuation of Rom. 9:5',[8] to which Professor Dunn refers but the detailed arguments of which he makes no attempt to rebut. Other recent commentators have given their support to the reference to Christ,[9] and – what is perhaps the most important recent development in this debate – the editors of the Nestle-Aland Greek New Testament, whose concern for thoroughly objective scholarship will hardly be impugned, have in the twenty-sixth edition (1979) substituted a comma after σάρκα for the colon of the previous edition. It is surely not unreasonable to suggest that at the present time the *onus probandi* rests squarely on the shoulders of those who reject the reference of v. 5b to Christ. We regard as by far the most probable explanation of v. 5 as a whole that which understands it to be affirming that Christ, who, in so far as his human existence is concerned, is of Jewish race, is also Lord over all things and by nature God blessed for ever, and therefore as strong evidence of Paul's belief in Christ's pre-existence and in the Incarnation.

The fifth passage is 10.6–10, with which Professor Dunn deals on pp. 184–7. He rejects the common interpretation of v. 6 ('But the righteousness which is of faith saith thus, Say not in thy heart, Who shall ascend into heaven? (that is, to bring Christ down:)') as referring to the Incarnation, arguing instead that Paul is thinking of heaven as the place where Christ is now, since his exaltation ('Christ may seem far away, inaccessible to earth-bound men, but the word of faith is near at hand' (p. 186)). But this interpretation, though Professor Dunn is of course not alone in maintaining it, does seem to be too much of a *tour de force*. One obvious difficulty in the way of accepting it is the order of vv. 6 and 7. The fact that v. 7 refers explicitly to Christ's resurrection from the dead makes it natural to suppose that what is referred to in v. 6 is likely to be something chronologically prior to the Resurrection. Professor Dunn's reply to this is that the order of the questions in vv. 6 and 7 was determined simply by Deuteronomy 30.12f. It is true that in Romans 10.9 we get a surprising order (outward confession

---

[8] In B. Lindars and S. S. Smalley (ed.), *Christ and Spirit in the New Testament: studies in honour of C. F. D. Moule*, Cambridge, 1973, pp. 95–112.

[9] E.g. H. Schlier, C. E. B. Cranfield.

mentioned before inward belief) and that the explanation of this seems to be Deuteronomy 30.14, in which 'in thy mouth' precedes 'in thy heart'. But in this case Paul immediately reverses the order in v. 10, so that the awkwardness is straightened out: nothing like this is done for the awkwardness presented (on Professor Dunn's interpretation) by the order of vv. 6 and 7. There is a further difficulty in the way of accepting Professor Dunn's interpretation: even if we can get over the obstacle of the order, there remains the difficulty that the parallelism between vv. 6 and 7 strongly suggests that, since what is spoken of in v. 7 has already happened, what is spoken of in v. 6 must also be something which has occurred already. A reference to bringing down the now exalted Christ from heaven combines very oddly with that to bringing up from the dead him whose resurrection is a fact of the past. The natural interpretation of v. 6 is surely that which understands it to refer to the Incarnation.

III

We turn now, in the third place, to a consideration of some of the features of Romans, the bearing of which on the subject of his inquiry Professor Dunn does not acknowledge but which seem to have a very strong claim to be taken into account.

Professor Dunn refrains from giving a separate treatment of the title 'Lord' on the ground that 'it denotes Christ's exalted (i.e. post-Easter) glory'.[10] But Paul's use of the title can hardly be without some bearing on the question whether he believed in Christ's pre-existence and in the Incarnation or not. That he must have been well acquainted both with the common secular uses of the word κύριος and also with its use in pagan religions is clear. But, if it is right to say that its use in the Septuagint (more than six thousand times) to represent the divine name YHWH is the key to the understanding of Paul's use of it with reference to Christ (and the fact that he applied to Christ, without – apparently – the least sense of inappropriateness, the κύριος of Septuagint passages in

---

[10] Pp. 271f, note 33 to chapter I.

which it is perfectly clear that the κύριος referred to is God himself[11] would seem to be very strong support for this view), then Paul's use of the title with reference to Christ must surely mean that, for him, the exalted Christ shares the name, the majesty, the authority, the deity, of the living God himself. But a necessary implication of this is that Paul believed in Christ's pre-existence and in the Incarnation. On any other assumption than this, the use of the title κύριος of Christ in the way in which Paul (someone who lived with, and, as it were, breathed, the Old Testament) used it, would surely be incomprehensible.

Strong confirmation of what has just been said about Paul's use of the title 'Lord' of the exalted Christ is afforded by the fact that he countenanced the offering of prayer to Christ. Evidence of this in Romans is to be seen in 10.12–14. In each of these three verses reference is made to 'calling upon' the Lord or the name of the Lord. That the Lord referred to is Christ is clear from the context. The Greek ἐπικαλεῖσθαι (rendered here in the RV by 'call upon') is a technical term for invoking in prayer.[12] That Paul, who certainly had not abandoned his commitment to the first two commandments of the Decalogue (to have done so would surely have been perceived by him as downright apostasy), could countenance prayer to Christ is something which has often not received the attention it deserves. Its significance cannot be neatly confined to the subject of how Paul thought about the exalted Christ; for only the one true living God can be rightly invoked in prayer, and, if the exalted Christ is one to whom prayer may rightly be addressed, then he must have been true God from all eternity. The idea of apotheosis was acceptable to pagans of the centuries before and after Christ, but to one who has lived in the light of the Old Testament can it be anything but a nonsense? To grasp the full significance of Paul's acceptance of the rightness of praying to

[11] E.g. Romans 10.13: for other examples reference may be made to my ICC commentary on Romans, pp. 529 and 839.

[12] Cf. W. Bauer, *Griechisch-deutsches Wörterbuch zu den Schriften des Neuen Testaments*, Berlin, 1971 corrected reprint of 5th ed. of 1958, s.v. ἐπικαλέω 2.b and see also 1a. Cf. Paul's use of '[those] that call upon the name of our Lord Jesus Christ' as a designation of Christians in 1 Corinthians 1.2.

Christ, one needs to consider Exodus 20.2–6 and Deuteronomy 5.7–10, and along with them such passages as Deuteronomy 6.4 (cf. Rom. 3.30); 11.16; Isaiah 42.8; Matthew 4.10; Mark 12.29, 32.

There is a rich variety of other ways in which Paul associates Christ with God with an uninhibitedness, which may easily be passed over unnoticed because it has become so familiar, but which, as soon as we stop to reflect on the implications of what we are reading, can hardly fail to strike us as utterly extraordinary and astonishing. Thus in 1.7 the source from which grace and peace are desired for the Roman Christians is 'God our Father and the Lord Jesus Christ'; and there is a suggestive parallel between 'The grace of our Lord Jesus Christ be with you', which is the *subscriptio* to the letter (16.20), and the prayer-wish of 15.33, 'Now the God of peace be with you all. Amen'.[13] In 8.35 and 39 'the love of Christ' and 'the love of God, which is in Christ Jesus our Lord' are used, respectively, in two closely corresponding contexts. The phrase 'the churches of Christ' in 16.16 answers to 'the churches of God' in 1 Corinthians 11.16. There is an interesting parallel between 'the gospel of God' in 15.16 and 'the gospel of Christ' in 15.19, though the two genitives are of different kinds, as is also the case in 1.1 ('separated unto the gospel of God') and 1.9 ('whom I serve in my spirit in the gospel of his Son'). In chapter 1 Paul makes it clear that 'the gospel of God' (v. 1), for the proclamation of which he has been set apart, is the gospel 'concerning . . . Jesus Christ our Lord' (vv. 3–4), that it is God's saving power (v. 16), and that in its being proclaimed both the gift of a status of righteousness before God (so I understand 'a righteousness of God' here) and also God's wrath are being revealed (vv. 17 and 18). According to 2.16, 'God' is going to carry out his eschatological judgment of men 'by Jesus Christ'.

Of special interest is the association of Christ with God in relation to faith. There are places where faith is spoken of explicitly as in God. So in 4.3 Paul quotes Genesis 15.6, 'And Abraham believed God . . . (ἐπίστευσεν . . . τῷ θεῷ): that is a giving

---

[13] On the 'God be with' formula reference may be made to my ICC commentary on Romans, p. 780.

credence to God's word, God's promise (cf. 4.17–21). In 4.5 he speaks of one who 'believeth on [ἐπί with the accusative] him that justifieth the ungodly' (that is, of course, God). And in 4.24 he describes Christians as those 'who believe on [again ἐπί with the accusative] him that raised Jesus our Lord from the dead'. In other places Christ is equally explicitly indicated as the object of faith. Thus in 3.22 the righteousness referred to is defined as being 'through faith in Jesus Christ', while in 3.26 God is spoken of as justifying 'the man that hath faith in Jesus': in both these places the noun πίστις is used with an objective genitive. [The view that the genitives in these two verses are to be understood as possessive (or subjective) has in recent years gained considerable support; but see now Chapter 7 below.] The verb πιστεύειν is used with ἐπί and the dative in 9.33 and 10.11 in the Septuagint quotation and with εἰς in 10.14 (expressly in the first relative clause: εἰς is no doubt also to be supplied in the second question, where οὗ stands for εἰς ἐκεῖνον οὗ). In all three verses Paul is thinking of Christ as the one believed in. There are also many occurrences both of πίστις and of πιστεύειν where no object of faith is mentioned and yet the existence of an object of faith is surely implied. To attempt to decide in each place whether God or Christ would more naturally be supposed to be the unspecified object would surely be unrealistic and inappropriate. The right conclusion to draw, I suspect, is – and, if this is true, then it is of the greatest importance for the subject of our inquiry – that, for Paul, faith in God and faith in Christ are inextricably bound together. Occurrences of πίστις to be mentioned here are in 1.5, 8, 12, 17; 3.25, 27, 30, 31; 5.1, 2; 9.30, 32; 10.6, 8, 17; 11.20; 12.3 (if my understanding of μέτρον πίστεως is right), 6; 16.26; and of πιστεύειν in 1.16, 3.22; 10.4; 13.11, 15.13.[14]

Two other matters fall to be mentioned just here. The first is that there is a close relationship between faith and hope in the Bible, and that, though ἐλπίς and ἐλπίζειν occur much less

---

[14] On the various meanings of πίστις and πιστεύειν in the Pauline epistles reference may be made to my ICC commentary on Romans, pp. 697f. See also pages referred to in index II, under πιστεύειν and πίστις and in Index III, under 'faith'.

frequently in Romans than do πίστις and πιστεύειν, there is perhaps enough of a hint of the possibility of discerning a similar pattern implicit in the use of the former pair of words in the epistle to that which we have seen in the use of the latter, to be worth noting.

The second matter is that there is a great deal of material in the Old Testament which makes the point that only God is the proper object of faith or hope in the fullest and deepest senses of the words. To put absolute faith or hope in any one or in anything but the one true God is idolatry. Out of many passages which could be cited it will be enough here to mention just a few (in each case indicating the words or expressions used in the LXX for faith or hope): Psalms 22.4, 5 [LXX: 21.5, 6]: 'Our fathers trusted in thee: they trusted, and thou didst deliver them . . . they trusted in thee, and were not ashamed' (ἐλπίζειν three times, twice with ἐπί and dative); 27 [26].13 (where the LXX has πιστεύω τοῦ ἰδεῖν τὰ ἀγαθὰ κυρίου ἐν γῇ ζώντων); 31.14 [LXX:30.15]: 'But I trusted in thee, O LORD: I said, Thou art my God' (ἐλπίζειν with ἐπί and accusative); 38.15 [LXX: 37.16]: 'For in thee, O LORD, do I hope: thou wilt answer, O LORD, my God' (ἐλπίζειν with ἐπί and dative); 78 [LXX: 77].22: (God was wroth with Israel) 'Because they believed not in God, and trusted not in his salvation' (πιστεύειν ἐν and ἐλπίζειν with ἐπί and accusative); 118 [LXX: 117] 8, 9: 'It is better to trust in the LORD than to put confidence in man. It is better to trust in the LORD than to put confidence in princes' (πεποιθέναι with ἐπί and accusative twice in v. 8, ἐλπίζειν with ἐπί and accusative twice in v. 9); 146 [LXX: 145].3, 5: 'Put not your trust in princes, nor in the son of man, in whom there is no help . . . Happy is the man that hath the God of Jacob for his help, whose hope is in the LORD his God' (πεποιθέναι with ἐπί and accusative, and ἡ ἐλπὶς αὐτοῦ also with ἐπί and accusative); Proverbs 3.5: 'Trust in the LORD with all thine heart, and lean not upon thine own understanding' (εἶναι πεποιθώς with ἐπί and dative); Isaiah 7.9: 'If ye will not believe, surely ye shall not be established' (πιστεύειν: it is faith in God that is in question); Jeremiah 17.5, 7: 'Cursed is the man that trusteth in man, and maketh flesh his arm, and whose heart departeth from

64

the LORD . . . Blessed is the man that trusteth in the LORD, and whose hope the LORD is' (τὴν ἐλπίδα ἔχειν with ἐπί and accusative, πεποιθέναι with ἐπί and dative, and ἐλπίς).

It seems to me that what is said in Romans about faith is (when it is seen in the light of the wealth of relevant Old Testament material of which only a few examples have been given above) further strong evidence of the author's conviction of Christ's oneness with God, and so of his eternity – and so of the author's belief in Christ's pre-existence and in the Incarnation.

Yet further evidence is provided by the passages concerning Christ's death for us. Its full weight can be measured accurately only when all the relevant passages are seen together,[15] but 5.8 and 3.24–26 will, I think, suffice to make the point which has to be made here. The assertion in 5.8 that God proves his own love for us by the fact that Christ died for us while we were still sinners is not to be explained as merely referring to a specially outstanding instance of the general truth that a man who performs an act of self-sacrificial love for his fellow-men affords a pointer to God's love and care for them. It is so solemnly and emphatically expressed (note the emphatic ἑαυτοῦ and the fact that the subject of the action described in the main clause is God), besides being an integral part of a context dealing with our reconciliation (that is, of God's transforming us from being his enemies into being his friends), that it surely cannot be convincingly explained as implying anything less than that Paul believed that in Christ's giving himself in death God was himself involved not just in sympathy but in person. A clue to the right understanding of the other passage is, I believe, afforded by the recognition that the καί in 3.26 is adverbial, that is, that it means not 'and' but 'even', so that the latter half of the verse may be translated 'so that he might be righteous even in justifying the man who believes in Jesus'. Paul is indicating that God's object was to justify sinners, who put their trust in Jesus, righteously, that is, in a way altogether worthy of himself as the merciful and loving God, who, because he truly and faithfully loves men, cannot condone their sin or allow it to appear

---

[15] For a list of these see ICC *Romans*, pp. 826–33.

as other than it is. In order so to forgive, without cruelly betraying his whole creation by compromising his own righteousness, God purposed that Christ should be a propitiatory sacrifice (3.25), that is, surely, purposed to direct against his own very self in his Son the full weight of that righteous wrath which men deserve. If – and only if – Jesus Christ is essentially one with the eternal God (and this carries with it pre-existence and incarnation), this passage makes sense, sense consonant with the character of God disclosed in Scripture.

In the light of what has just been said, must we not conclude that, when he refers to Christ as 'Son of God' in 1.4, 'his [that is, God's] Son' in 1.3, 9; 5.10; 8.29, 'his [that is, God's] own [ἑαυτοῦ] Son' in 8.3, 'his [that is, God's] own [ἰδίου] Son' in 8.32, and to God as 'the God and Father of our Lord Jesus Christ' in 15.6 (cf. 'the Father' in 6.4), Paul intends to indicate a relationship which involves a real community of nature between Christ and God? The ἑαυτοῦ and ἰδίου in 8.3 and 32, respectively, seem to be used to underline the contrast between the one true Son of God by nature and the sons by adoption.

But the evidence of Romans seems to take us still farther. There are a number of short passages each containing a combination of references to God (the Father), to Christ, to the Spirit, in close proximity to each other, which, taken together, seem to me to constitute a very strong basis for the affirmation that, though no explicit formulation of a doctrine of the Trinity is to be seen in the epistle, the theology of the author of Romans is essentially Trinitarian. The following must be set out:[16]

> (i) 1.1–4 ('Paul, slave of Christ Jesus, . . . set apart for *the work of proclaiming* God's message of good news, which he promised beforehand . . . , concerning his Son, who was born of David's seed according to the flesh, who was appointed Son of God in power according to the Spirit of holiness from the resurrection of the dead, even Jesus Christ our Lord').

[16] I quote these passages according to the translation in my ICC commentary, by permission of T. & T. Clark.

(ii) 5.1–5 ('. . . we have peace with God through our Lord Jesus Christ, . . . we exult in hope of the glory of God . . . And this hope does not put us to shame, for God's love has been poured out in our hearts through the Holy Spirit who has been given to us').

(iii) 8.1–4 ('So then there is now no condemnation for those who are in Christ Jesus. For the law of the Spirit of life has in Christ Jesus set thee free from the law of sin and of death. For God, having sent his own Son in the likeness of sinful flesh and to deal with sin, condemned sin in the flesh . . . , so that the righteous requirement of the law might be fulfilled in us who do not walk according to the flesh but according to the Spirit').

(iv) 8.9 ('But you are not in the flesh but in the Spirit, seeing that God's Spirit dwells in you. (If someone does not possess Christ's Spirit, then he does not belong to Christ)').

(v) 8.11 ('But, if the Spirit of him who raised Jesus from the dead dwells in you, he who raised from the dead Christ Jesus shall quicken your mortal bodies also through his Spirit who dwells in you').

(vi) 8.16f ('The Spirit himself assures our spirit that we are children of God. And if children, then also heirs: heirs of God and fellow heirs of Christ, seeing that we are *now* suffering with him, in order that we may *hereafter* be glorified with him').

(vii) 14.17f ('For the kingdom of God is not eating and drinking, but righteousness and peace and joy in the Holy Spirit; for he who therein serves Christ is well-pleasing to God and deserves men's approval').

(viii) 15.16 ('to be a minister of Christ Jesus unto the Gentiles, serving God's message of good news with a holy service, in order that the offering consisting of the Gentiles may be acceptable, having been sanctified by the Holy Spirit').

(ix) 15.30 ('I exhort you [, brothers] by our Lord Jesus Christ and by the love of the Spirit to join earnestly with me in prayers on my behalf to God').

But more significant than the simple fact that passages occur in which God, Christ and the Spirit are mentioned together, is what is ascribed (whether explicitly or implicitly) to Christ and to the Spirit not only in these passages but also in many other places throughout the epistle. It seems to me that Paul is thinking of Christ and the Spirit as effecting (for example, in justification and sanctification) what only the one true God himself can be seriously thought of as effecting – things, which, if they are not done by the eternal God himself (and none other), are just not done at all. If this reading of Romans is correct, then the whole structure of theological thought which has shaped and ordered it must surely be acknowledged to have a Trinitarian character.

The conclusion to be drawn from the evidence of Romans is surely, *pace* Professor Dunn, that its author firmly believed in the pre-existence of Christ, in the sense that as Son of God he has shared the divine life from all eternity, and in the Incarnation, in the sense that at a particular time the eternal Son of God assumed our human nature for the sake of humankind and of the whole creation. My impression is that the author of *Christology in the Making* – for all the valuable provocativeness of the contribution he has made, which is gratefully acknowledged – has not yet got the measure of the sheer intellectual power and alertness of the author of the Epistle to the Romans.

It is with painful awareness of their inadequacy for the purpose that the writer of these comments offers them as an expression of his gratitude to, and affection for, the distinguished scholar, to whose memory this essay is dedicated.

6

Preaching on Romans

The practice of preaching through biblical books section by section, in order, can be, I have long believed, if followed intelligently and sensitively, enormously beneficial to the church. The purpose of this essay is to make some suggestions on how it might be followed with the Epistle to the Romans, the book which Luther wanted all Christians to learn by heart. The careful structure of Romans makes continuous exposition particularly appropriate and rewarding.

It is clear that even a very long series of sermons would not exhaust the riches of Romans. But I think it is a reasonable thing to attempt to expound it in twenty-four sermons of not more than half an hour (a series of thirty-two sermons, which is what John Chrysostom gave on Romans, is probably rather long for an ordinary congregation). One would obviously be able to come back again at a later stage. It is probably, in most circumstances, not feasible to involve both morning and evening services in such a series. One substantial break would seem to be desirable, and, since Romans 1–8 and 9–16 need about the same length of treatment (Chrysostom, for example, preached sixteen sermons on 1–8 and sixteen on 9–16), the natural place for it would seem to be between 8.39 and 9.1. Maybe two or three short breaks would also help; but one should particularly avoid having such a break within Romans 9–11, and, I think, also Romans 6–8.

* First published in *The Expository Times* 99 (1987–88), pp. 36–40. This article was based on a lecture given in New College, Edinburgh, on 5 November 1986, at the invitation of Professor J. C. O'Neill.

I suggest a division of the epistle as follows: (1) 1.1–7; (2) 1.8–16a; (3) 1.16b–17; (4) 1.18–32; (5) 2.1–3.20; (6) 3.21–26; (7) 3.27–4.25; (8) 5.1–21; (9) 6.1–23; (10) 7.1–25; (11) 8.1–16; (12) 8.17–39; (13) 9.1–29; (14) 9.30–10.21; (15) 11.1–36; (16) 12.1–2; (17) 12.3–8; (18) 12.9–21; (19) 13.1–7; (20) 13.8–10; (21) 13.11–14; (22) 14.1–15.13; (23) 15.14–33; (24) 16.1–27. I can only offer suggestions about a few of these sections here,[1] but I hope it may possibly be enough to encourage some readers who have to make sermons every week.

In the first sermon one could take two or three minutes to indicate by way of introduction the occasion and date of the epistle, where St Paul was, and his use of the opening formula of a Greek or Latin letter. After that I would concentrate on just three fairly straightforward points. First, Paul describes, defines, both himself (vv. 1–6) and those whom he is addressing (v. 7a) by reference to the gospel. The really important thing about himself and about them is, in Paul's view, the truth which the gospel declares. Do we so understand ourselves and our fellow human beings? And are we beginning to live as people who have this understanding? Secondly, what Paul desires for the Christians in Rome is grace and peace. What does he mean by those two words? As he uses them they sum up the gift of God in Christ. Do we desire for ourselves and those whom we love this grace and this peace above all things? Thirdly, what Paul thought about Jesus is indicated by the fact that he associated the Lord Jesus Christ with God our Father in this striking way as the source from which he looked for this grace and peace. (Verse 7b gives us a lead with regard to the interpretation of the difficult vv. 3 and 4. How deeply one should go into them would depend on the congregation.)

In (2), 1.8–16a, the fact that Paul is humble enough to expect to receive as well as to give (v. 12) is a vitally important word for ministers and congregations alike about the true nature of pastoral care in the church of Christ, a reminder that it is meant to be the

---

[1] I have tried to expound the epistle in *A Critical and Exegetical Commentary on the Epistle to the Romans*, Edinburgh, 1, [6]1987; 2 [4]1986, and (without use of Greek) *Romans: a Shorter Commentary*, Edinburgh, [2]1986.

mutual consolation of brothers and sisters, a truth very often ignored to the grievous impoverishment and weakening of the church. Paul regards himself as a debtor to the Gentiles (v. 14), not as having received some benefit from them, but as having been appointed by God to do something for them. We owe to our fellow human beings as a debt that which God has commanded us to be or do for them or to give to them. Paul's 'For I am not ashamed of the gospel' reflects his recognition of the fact that the gospel is something of which, in this world, Christians will always be tempted to be ashamed. Alas for the Christian who has not learned to reckon with this fact! Indeed the business of living the Christian life is to a very large extent that of resisting the temptation to be ashamed of the gospel, which is always with us, because of the world's hostility to Christ and because in the town called Vanity and its ancient fair the gospel seems so weak and vulnerable and poor, so altogether unimpressive. And it is well to remember that there is a very wide variety of ways in which one can be ashamed of the gospel.

(3), 1.16b–17, states the theme of what is to follow and is of fundamental importance for the understanding of the whole epistle. Here it will be particularly important for the intending preacher to work at his commentaries conscientiously and intelligently, and not be content till the direct relevance of this verse-and-a-half to himself and his congregation becomes luminous for him.

In (4), 1.18–32, the reference to God's wrath is liable to offend. But ordinary people can usually see that a good man will react to cruelty, injustice, falsehood, with indignation. Our human 'righteous indignation' is always sadly compromised. God's wrath is an expression of his love. He is wroth with our sinfulness precisely because he loves us truly and seriously and faithfully. His wrath is being revealed now in the preaching because it was revealed in the cross. The last part of v. 18 is a remarkably illuminating definition of sin. Sin is always an assault on God's truth, an attempt to conceal, suppress, obliterate the reality of God as Creator, Redeemer and Judge, an attempt which is bound to prove futile.

71

To give four sermons to chapter 1 may seem over-generous, but in expounding a book one often does need to allow more time for the early part – afterwards one can take some things for granted as having already been explained. (5), 2.1–3.20, is an awful lot for one sermon and calls for rather different treatment from that which is appropriate for a shorter text. Its function in the argument is clear enough. 1.18–32 has spoken of the judgment pronounced by the gospel on humankind as a whole: the purpose of 2.1–3.20 is to make it clear that the Jews, who might think themselves exempt from God's judgment, are in fact no exception. They too are sinners. But the points made against the Jews of Paul's day in the four paragraphs, 2.1–11, 12–16, 17–24 and 25–29, can all be applied *mutatis mutandis* to Christians. We need to hear in them warnings not to store up judgment for ourselves by judging others self-righteously, not to imagine that merely knowing the will of God is in itself security, not to close our eyes to the shameful inconsistencies in our own lives, not to cherish a wrong sort of reliance on the fact of our membership of the church. In the flow of 2.1–3.20 the eight verses 3.1–8 are parenthetic, the first four of them guarding against a possible misunderstanding of what Paul has been saying as implying that the Jew has no advantage at all and that there is no profit at all in circumcision. That would be a serious misunderstanding, and, against it, Paul has to insist that man's unfaithfulness does not annul God's faithfulness to his word. Verses 5–8 are then a kind of parenthesis within a parenthesis, guarding against a possible misunderstanding of vv. 1–4. With v. 9 we are back to the main thrust of the section, the demonstration that all human beings are sinners (Jesus alone excepted) and there is no question of anyone's being righteous before God except only by faith.

It would be important to make it clear that what Paul is seeking to establish in (5), far from being just a matter of intellectual theological correctness, has a direct bearing on the attitudes of Christians to God, to their neighbours and to themselves, and so on the whole of their daily living. The Christian who forgets that he is among his fellow human beings as a fellow-sinner who can have no righteous status before God otherwise than by God's utterly undeserved mercy, will certainly not live a truly Christian life. Mr Bradshaw in Elizabeth Gaskell's novel *Ruth* is a memorable example of what happens – a Victorian example, but he has plenty of late twentieth-century equivalents.

(6), 3.21–26, is, I believe, the heart of the whole epistle. There would be no gift of a righteous status before God revealed and made available in the preaching of the gospel, had not that gift been once for all revealed and made available in the gospel events themselves. These verses look back to those events. The text falls naturally into three parts: vv. 21–23, 24 and 25–26.

In the first part the initial 'But now' points to the decisiveness of what was accomplished in the gospel events, emphasizing the contrast between the situation before and the situation after those events. Both in v. 21 and in v. 22 'righteousness' denotes the status of righteousness before God given by God. It has been manifested 'apart from the law' in the sense that it has not been earned by human obedience to the law; but it is attested 'by the law and the prophets'. It has to be accepted as a gift 'through faith in Jesus Christ', and it is for all who will believe, without distinction.

In the second part (v. 24) 'freely' and 'by his grace' support each other, the latter phrase pointing to the source of human beings' justification in the undeserved mercy of God. Whether the thought of a ransom price was present in Paul's mind when he used the word 'redemption' is not certain. What is certain is that his language implies that the believer's righteous status has been brought about by a definite and altogether decisive action by God. What emerges here is that the centre, the heart, of the gospel is a particular deed of God accomplished once for all in Christ on behalf of humanity (and indeed of God's whole creation), some-thing objective, independent of us human beings who make up the church, and of our feelings, our comprehension, our aspirations, our deserts. Too often our church life and our church services give a quite different impression – that our religion is a subjective matter, concerned with our feelings and vague aspirations and the transient tastes and sensations of the moment more than with the living God's saving deed and all that follows from it. This verse seems to me to point the way to the real renewal of our worship and our church life.

The third part of this text (vv. 25–26) is saying, if I understand it aright, that God, because in his mercy he willed to forgive sinners and because, being truly merciful, he willed to forgive them righteously, that is, without in any way condoning their sin, purposed to take upon himself in the person of his Son the full weight of that righteous, holy wrath which they would deserve. It would be for sinners to appropriate the precious benefit of that costly divine act by faith, accepting it trustingly, humbly, gratefully. In vv. 25 and 26 'righteousness' refers to God's own moral righteousness, and similarly the adjective 'just' (RV) in v. 26. God's righteousness, laid open to question by his passing over of sins in his forbearance, was to be proved by the cross. The latter part of v. 26 affords a most precious insight into the meaning of the cross, as Paul understood it. If we recognize that the Greek word *kai*, which can mean either 'and' or 'even', is here used in the sense 'even' ('that he might be righteous even in justifying the man who believes in Jesus'), the significance of the clause stands out more sharply; but, if we insist on the translation 'and', the sense of the half-verse must still be the same, though less clearly expressed: namely, that God might justify righteously, without compromising his own righteousness, the sinner who trusts in Jesus. The cross is about real, serious, costly forgiveness. God does not cruelly insult his creature man with a cheap forgiveness denying the seriousness of sin. To have done that would have been to violate his goodness and abandon his love.

The experience which perhaps more than any other illuminated this for me was a visit to a German prisoner of war camp in London in the afternoon of Boxing Day 1945. That afternoon I went to a special camp known as the London Prisoner of War 'Cage', hoping to hold a service for Christmas; but the commandant explained that the current inmates could not be allowed to mix together, as they were all either people suspected of being war criminals or else people needed as witnesses in connection with war crimes, but that he would send round to each room to inquire who would like to be visited by a British Protestant army chaplain. So I spent my

74

afternoon visiting the different rooms, not knowing who was a suspected perpetrator of a war crime and who was merely a witness to such a crime, and praying with those I visited. It was an experience which made Romans 3.25–26 live for me.

In preparing to preach on (9), 6.1–23, (10), 7.1–25, (11), 8.1–16, and (12), 8.17–39, it will be helpful to consider the three chapters together; for, taken closely together, they give a balanced and profound account of sanctification, whereas, understood in isolation from one another, they can be seriously misleading. In 6.1–23 Paul seems to presuppose a degree of theological sophistication in the Roman Christians which one could not take for granted in an average congregation. He assumes, apparently, some awareness on their part of one at least of the four senses of the believer's dying with Christ and being raised with him and a readiness to reckon with the rest of them. This fourfold dying and being raised with Christ is implicit throughout the chapter as the basis of the believer's obedience. We died and were raised with Christ in his death and resurrection in the sense that God has decided to regard his death and resurrection as 'for us'; we died and were raised with Christ in our baptism, because it was the pledge and seal given to us as individuals of that divine decision about us; we are obliged therefore to seek to die daily and hourly to sin and to allow ourselves daily and hourly to be raised up to newness of life; one day we shall die finally to sin in our dying and at the last we shall share in the resurrection of the dead. Such is the basis of the summons in vv. 12–14 to the 'glorious revolution' of the Christian life, the revolt against sin's usurping rule in the name of our rightful ruler, God.

Of Paul's awareness of the seriousness and the costliness of the conflict which that revolt involves and of his frank recognition of the fact that in this life it is never finished the latter part of Romans 7 is proof, if the view of Augustine, Aquinas, Luther, Calvin and many others that it refers to the Christian life (not the pre-conversion life) is accepted, as it surely should be. Thus understood vv. 14–25 bar the way to a complacent, triumphalistic interpretation of Romans 8, into which those who have taken the other view of 7.14ff have often fallen.

(11), 8.1–16, tells of the work of the Holy Spirit in the sanctification of believers. It is a work of liberation. The Holy Spirit, having begun to set us free by enabling us to put our trust in Christ, continues that work in us by giving us more and more freedom from ourselves, from the false god Ego, and for God and our neighbour. Sanctification means the growing freedom to obey God. It cannot be too much stressed that (11) does not point to any spectacular and exciting releases of pent-up religious or other emotions, to any exuberance of self-expression or even to what are elsewhere in the New Testament called 'mighty works', as the proof of the indwelling of God's Spirit, but, with sobering emphasis, to the fulfilment in the lives of those who walk according to the Spirit of the righteous requirement of the law. Sanctification is the fulfilment of the promise in Jeremiah 31.33 that God would put his law in his people's inward parts and write it on their hearts, that is, create in them a glad and free commitment to it, a wholehearted desire to obey it.

When in v. 15, Paul wants to sum up what fulfilling the righteous requirement of the law means, he speaks simply of calling God 'Father'; for to address the real God as 'Father', not casually, unthinkingly or hypocritically, but intelligently, responsibly, seriously, sincerely, carries with it everything the law requires. The freedom which the Spirit creates and sustains and increases is freedom to live as God's child.

And this life as God's child is, according to (12), 8.17–39, a life characterized by hope; for the children are also heirs looking forward to an inheritance. But this hope is no narrow, self-centred hope, but a generous, God-centred hope, which includes hope for all the creation (8.19–22). Its absolute certainty is underlined with striking eloquence in vv. 31–39.

(13), 9.1–29, (14), 9.30–10.21, (15), 11.1–36, are obviously important but also specially difficult. They need to be understood together. Paul's discussion of the problem of Israel's rejection of Christ should be heard to the end before one attempts to form an opinion about it. In a world in which the memory of the Holocaust is still for many fearfully vivid, in which fresh examples of crude and blatant antisemitism are quite often reported, in which unconscious prejudice is often insidiously at work, and in which, on the other hand, sympathy with the Jews in their past sufferings and a sense of guilt in connection with them are liable to express themselves in an uncritical support for the state of Israel which takes little or no account of the wrongs suffered by the Palestinians, the obligation on Christians to listen attentively to what these chapters have to say is surely unavoidable. It will be a strenuous adventure.

(19), 13.1–7, is also specially difficult, and congregations need help with it. The key to a right understanding is the realization that the Greek verb represented by AV 'be subject', RV 'be in subjection' is not equivalent to 'obey'. In ordinary English to obey someone is to do what that person commands. In Greek there are three very obvious verbs, all used in the New Testament, which convey this meaning. But Paul used another verb here. I think we can assume that he did so deliberately, because he thought it more suitable. It was not his intention to put a blank cheque in the hands of all civil rulers and authorities, laying on Christians the obligation to do whatever such authorities might command. And the Bible Societies and others who have used 'Obedience to Rulers' as a heading for this section have done a very serious – though no doubt unintentional – disservice to the church and to the cause of truth. The verb Paul uses here is used in Ephesians 5.21 of a reciprocal obligation ('subjecting yourselves one to another in the fear of Christ'). Obedience in the ordinary sense of the English word can hardly be reciprocal. What the Greek verb denotes is the recognition that another has a claim on one that takes precedence over one's own claim on oneself. To subject oneself to one's fellow-Christian is to recognize that his claim on one is superior to one's own claim on oneself, so to put his true interests before one's own. In exhorting the Roman Christians to be subject to the civil authorities Paul is reminding them that, as Christians, they have an inescapable obligation to the state, an inescapable political responsibility, laid on them by God, to be fulfilled conscientiously. The content of that obligation for Christians in the Roman empire of the first century has to be understood from the rest of what Paul says here and from other material in the New Testament. The

Christian who lives in late twentieth-century Britain has to translate this into the terms of the very different conditions of a democratic state. Since he has much more power to influence events, for him to fail to use that power or to use it unintelligently, irresponsibly or selfishly would be – in the phraseology of v. 2 – to withstand the ordinance of God. For example, to fail to try as hard as one can to be as fully and reliably informed about political issues as possible would be to withstand God's ordinance. That the church in Britain needs to hear sermons on Romans 13.1–7 is very clear; but it is important to realize that this passage is liable to be seriously and indeed disastrously misunderstood.

(20), 13.8–10 (on the debt which must constantly be paid but can never be discharged) is relatively easy to expound, though so difficult to heed. And (21), 13.11–14, is surely a text which cries out to be preached on, once one has escaped the mire of the notorious delay-of-the-Parousia problem.

One sermon for the whole of (22), 14.1–15.13, may seem absurd. But I think it is true to say that there is one main point that Paul is trying to make in this passage and therefore it makes sense (in a series of only twenty-four sermons on Romans) to concentrate on bringing out as clearly as possible that main point in its relevance to the church today. It is not at all easy to determine precisely what was at issue between the 'weak' and the 'strong', and different explanations are offered. My guess is that the weak were Christians (mainly Jewish Christians presumably) who, while (unlike the Judaizers to whom Galatians refers) neither thinking they were putting God in their debt by their observance nor wanting to force all Christians to conform to their way, yet felt strongly that, as far as they themselves were concerned, they could not give up the observance of the ceremonial requirements of the Old Testament law with a clear conscience. The strong, on the other side, were Christians who had recognized that now that he, who is the very substance of the law, the One to whom all along its ceremonies had been pointing, has come, it is no longer necessary to obey the ceremonial requirements literally. Paul himself agreed with the position of the strong (in 15.1 he counts himself among them – 'we that are strong'), while disapproving of the lack of sensitivity towards the weak which many of them displayed. He recognized the special vulnerability of the weak. If they were driven by ridicule or other social pressure in the church to act in violation of what they strongly (even if in a not very well-thought-through manner) believed to be for them the right expression of their faith in Christ, they would be grieved and damaged in their inmost life, their very integrity as human beings would be destroyed. So Paul's exhortation in this part of his letter was directed mainly towards the strong, to try to persuade them to be ready, for the sake of their weak brothers' welfare, to forgo the outward expression of their inward liberty, good though it was in itself – though he also warns the weak against being censorious of the strong.

There is probably no situation in the church today exactly analogous to that which Paul was addressing, and it would be a rash man who would claim to know for certain the exact nature of the situation addressed by Paul. But the essential message in this passage is, I think, clear enough; and my impression is that it is a message which the church of today sorely needs to hear and to heed. Paul insists on the seriousness of causing a brother or sister for whom Christ died to stumble, that is, of putting at risk or destroying his or her existence as a believer. Of the many issues over which Christians today are divided, both between and within the various denominations, there are certainly some with regard to which the consciences of individual Christians are very deeply involved. Where that is so, the danger is often very great that those who are in the majority will fail to show proper respect for the consciences of their brothers and sisters who are in the minority. The church today in Britain and elsewhere surely needs to listen hard to this passage, lest in our arrogance and thoughtless selfishness we treat as cheap what was bought by Christ at great cost.

(24), 16.1–27, seems at first sight very barren, consisting largely of names, many of them unfamiliar. But that first impression would be wrong. Here we get a glimpse of Phoebe, a deacon (the discriminatory term 'deaconess' had not yet appeared!) of the church in Cenchreae, and of that ecclesiastical office, which later generations (even in the Reformed churches) have so sadly diminished, tending to be more concerned about power than about service. We get a glimpse of the Christians in Rome, meeting apparently in a number of different groups in private houses. There is a warning in vv. 17–20, which an ordinary modern congregation can profitably ponder, and the doxology of vv. 25–27, though hardly of Paul's composition, can still illumine and edify. But the most surprising thing, especially to any one who knows something about the position of women in Judaism and in the Graeco-Roman world of the first century, is the prominence of women in this chapter. There is Phoebe who is to bear Paul's letter to Rome and deliver it to the Christians there. And in the list of greetings in vv. 3–15, a long list because Paul wanted to establish as many points of contact as possible in the great city which he had not yet visited, of the twenty-six individuals specified (twenty-four named and two otherwise identified, namely, Rufus's mother and Nereus's sister) seventeen are male and nine female, according to the AV. (I mention the AV, because it rightly takes *Iounian* in v. 7 to be the accusative of the feminine name Junia, whereas the RV and various other more recent translations and many commentators have treated it as the accusative of a supposed masculine name Junias, which is not otherwise known, on the ground that a female apostle is unthinkable.) Nine out of twenty-six is something over 33.3%, which it is interesting to compare with the percentage of members of an average General Assembly or General Synod who are women. Notable also are the use of the verb 'labour' three times with reference to particular women (Paul uses it elsewhere of his own apostolic labours), the description of Junia in v. 7 as outstanding among the apostles and the fact that Prisca is mentioned before her husband in v. 3. Here too there is something for the church of today to heed.

7

On the Πίστις Χριστοῦ Question

The revival of the suggestion that Ἰησοῦ Χριστοῦ in Romans 3.22 and similar genitives in v. 26; Galatians 2.16a, 16b, 20; 3.22 and Philippians 3.9 should be understood as subjective rather than objective has gathered pace in the course of the last twenty years.[1]

The Greek word πίστις can mean 'faith' in the sense of belief, trust; it can also mean 'faithfulness'. Some supporters of the subjective genitive interpretation have favoured the former, and some the latter, as its meaning in the phrases under consideration, while others seem to have hesitated between the two or thought to combine them, using such expressions as 'Christ's own faith/faithfulness'. It may be said at once that neither 'the faith of Christ' nor 'the faithfulness of Christ' can be simply ruled out as incompatible with the thinking of the early church as it is reflected in the New Testament. That he who had taught his disciples about prayer, teaching them to address God as 'Father' and to trust his fatherly care of them, and who had himself spent long periods in prayer, had faith in God may well have seemed obvious. And, as to

---

[1] See, e.g., L. T. Johnson, 'Rom 3.21–26 and the Faith of Jesus' in *CBQ* 44 (1982), pp. 77–90; R. B. Hays, *The Faith of Jesus Christ: an investigation of the narrative substructure of Galatians 3:1–4:11*, Chicago, 1983; S. K. Williams, 'Again Pistis Christou', in *CBQ* 49 (1987), pp. 431–47; M. D. Hooker, ΠΙΣΤΙΣ ΧΡΙΣΤΟΥ, in *NTS* 35 (1989), pp. 321–42 (republished in her *From Adam to Christ: essays on Paul*, Cambridge, 1990, pp. 165–86); B. W. Longenecker, 'Πίστις in Rom. 3.25: neglected evidence for the "Faithfulness of Christ"?', in *NTS* 39 (1993), pp. 478–80; I. G. Wallis, *The Faith of Jesus Christ in early Christian Traditions*, Cambridge, 1995.

his faithfulness, it would be easy to cite New Testament passages which attest his having been faithful to God, to his mission from God, to his own people Israel, to sinful humanity generally, and also his continuing faithfulness as our High Priest, as well as his being the expression of God's own faithfulness. The question we are now concerned with is whether in the occurrences of πίστις which have been listed Paul had in mind either of these things.

I want first to take up a hint dropped by Joseph A. Fitzmyer in his fine Romans commentary of 1993.[2] He asks the question, 'Does the vb. *pisteuein* ever have Christ as the subject in the NT?' He does not follow this up – perhaps because he judged that his case was convincing enough without this further piece of evidence. But his question is pertinent. According to the 'Häufigkeitsindex' in Kurt Aland's *Vollständige Konkordanz zum griechischen Neuen Testament*, Band II,[3] p. 407, πιστεύειν ties with πίστις (by a curious coincidence both words occur the same number of times) and μέγας as the sixty-fifth most common word in the New Testament. It occurs 243 times. Unless one accepts the not very likely suggestion that in Mark 9.23 τῷ πιστεύοντι refers to Jesus, there are only two occurrences where Jesus is the subject of the verb. One is John 2.24, where the verb is transitive and does not denote faith ('But Jesus did not trust himself unto them, for that he knew all men'); the other is 1 Timothy 3.16, where it is used in the passive voice (ὃς ... ἐπιστεύθη ἐν κόσμῳ). It has been suggested that in 2 Corinthians 4.13 Paul, in quoting LXX Psalm 115.1 [English versions: 116.10], was thinking of the psalm as messianic, and that there is here a reference to Jesus' faith;[4] but we can scarcely claim that ἐπίστευσα here is an occurrence of the verb with Jesus as the subject. In at least 239 of the 243 occurrences

[2] J. A. Fitzmyer, *Romans: A New Translation with Introduction and Commentary*, New York, 1993, p. 345. J. D. G. Dunn, 'Once More ΠΙΣΤΙΣ ΧΡΙΣΤΟΥ', in E. H. Lovering (ed.), *Society of Biblical Literature 1991 Seminar Papers*, Atlanta, 1991, p. 732, n. 12, had already noted 'the absence of the verbal equivalent . . . , i.e. "Christ believed"'.

[3] Berlin, New York, 1978.

[4] A. T. Hanson, *Jesus Christ and the Old Testament*, London, 1965, pp. 145–7, followed by Hooker, *From Adam to Christ*, pp. 178–9.

of πιστεύειν there is no question at all of Jesus' being the subject of the verb. And of the forty-two occurrences of this verb in the seven epistles generally agreed to be by Paul (Romans, 1 and 2 Corinthians, Galatians, Philippians, 1 Thessalonians and Philemon) 2 Corinthians 4.13 is the only one where Jesus' being the subject of the verb is remotely possible. In the absence of any clear statement that Jesus 'believed', 'had faith', it is surely difficult to accept that Jesus' faith was as important for Paul or for the early church generally as some recent writers have maintained. The above statistical evidence, while by itself not a conclusive disproof of the explanation of the πίστις Χριστοῦ passages as referring to Jesus' faith, is surely, at the least, an extremely large question mark placed against it.

We may also note at this point that of the eighty-four occurrences of πίστις in the seven epistles, that is, of those which are left when the seven with which we are specially concerned have been excluded, there is none in which there is a clear reference either to the faith or to the faithfulness of Christ, while in none of the remaining 152 instances of πίστις in the New Testament is the reference clearly to Christ's own faith or faithfulness, though the possibility that a reference to it is implicit in Hebrews 12.2 may be mentioned. With regard to πιστός the position is that it occurs nine times in the seven epistles. In one instance (1 Thess. 5.24) the reference is possibly to Christ but more probably to God. In the rest of the New Testament it occurs fifty-eight times; and in 2 Thessalonians 3.3; 2 Timothy 2.13; Hebrews 2.17; 3.2, 5/6; Revelation 1.5; 3.14 and 19.11 the reference is to Christ. Where the reference is to Christ the word is used in its sense of 'faithful'.

The foregoing statistics, while they suggest that in the New Testament apart from the πίστις Χριστοῦ passages there is slightly more evidence of interest in the thought of the faithfulness of Christ than in the thought of his faith, suggest very strongly that neither the thought of Jesus' faithfulness nor the thought of his faith was prominent in the thinking of the first-century church. When we set over against the absence of clear references to Jesus' πίστις or to his πιστεύειν and the paucity of references to his faithfulness such unambiguous references to faith in Christ as

John 3.16; 6.40; 14.1, 12; Acts 16.31; 19.4; Romans 10.11, 14; Galatians 2.16 (ἡμεῖς εἰς Χριστὸν Ἰησοῦν ἐπιστεύσαμεν); Ephesians 1.15; Philippians 1.29; Colossians 1.4; 2.5; 1 Peter 1.8; 1 John 5.10, 13, it is difficult to avoid the conclusion that the evidence so far considered is overwhelmingly in favour of accepting the objective genitive interpretation of the πίστις Χριστοῦ passages.

In what follows I shall pay special attention to Ian G. Wallis, *The Faith of Jesus Christ in early Christian Traditions*, Cambridge, 1995, as being one of the latest and also one of the most ambitious treatments of the subject.

Pages 69-72 of his book contain his discussion of the grammatical arguments which have been used in the πίστις Χριστοῦ debate. A. J. Hultgren may have overstated his case, when he claimed that, apart from the passages under discussion, whenever Paul uses πίστις with a genitive which is clearly to be understood as subjective, 'the article is invariably present';[5] but the fact remains that the article is at any rate almost always present in these cases, and its absence in the πίστις Χριστοῦ passages tells strongly in favour of the objective genitive interpretation. Wallis' attempts to weaken the force of this argument strike me as unconvincing.

The claim which he makes on p. 71 that, 'apart from Paul, there are no unambiguous cases in the New Testament where πίστις followed by Christ or God in the genitive case must be interpreted objectively' may be challenged. The injunction ἔχετε πίστιν θεοῦ in Mark 11.22 is surely as unambiguous a case as one could desire. To suggest, as Wallis does, that θεοῦ is a genitive of origin ('faith from God') is surely a desperate move. Three other examples are perhaps less clear, though I suspect that the genitive is in each of them objective. In each case the article is present before πίστις, and this leads J. D. G. Dunn (though he is a supporter of the objective genitive in the πίστις Χριστοῦ passages) to take these genitives as subjective.[6] In James 2.1 he takes τὴν πίστιν τοῦ κυρίου ἡμῶν Ἰησοῦ Χριστοῦ to mean 'the faith which our Lord Jesus Christ himself displayed'. But it is surely natural in the

---

[5] A. J. Hultgren, 'The *Pistis Christou* Formulation in Paul', in *NT* 22 (1980), p. 253.

[6] Dunn, op. cit., pp. 732–3.

context to understand μὴ ἐν προσωπολημψίαις ἔχετε τὴν πίστιν τοῦ κυρίου ἡμῶν Ἰησοῦ Χριστοῦ to mean 'do not try to combine the faith which you have in our Lord Jesus Christ with respect of persons'. I would suggest that the reason for the definite article here is not to signal a subjective genitive but to make the reference to faith more specific – not faith generally but the faith which those addressed are assumed to possess. In Revelation 2.13 οὐκ ἠρνήσω τὴν πίστιν μου surely more probably means 'you have not denied your faith in me' (the article having the force of 'your') than 'you have not denied my faith'. Similarly, in Revelation 14.12 οἱ τηροῦντες τὰς ἐντολὰς τοῦ θεοῦ καὶ τὴν πίστιν Ἰησοῦ would seem to mean 'those who keep the commandments of God and their faith in Jesus' (the article having the specifying force of 'their').

On p. 72 Wallis offers his translation of Romans 3.21–26, in which he represents διὰ πίστεως Ἰησοῦ Χριστοῦ in v. 22 by 'through Jesus Christ's faith' and τὸν ἐκ πίστεως Ἰησοῦ in v. 26 by 'the one [who lives] from Jesus' faith [or the one participating in Jesus' faith]', and also renders διὰ πίστεως in v. 25 as 'through [Jesus'] faith'. He raises the question whether, when Paul used the perfect passive of φανεροῦν in v. 21, 'the emphasis falls on the initial manifestation or [on the] subsequent "revelations" through the gospel' (p. 74), and suggests that many commentators who have understood Ἰησοῦ Χριστοῦ in v. 22 as objective have thereby been led to 'qualify this revelation in terms of human response and, by so doing, to come down on the side of the latter' (that is, on the side of taking the emphasis in πεφανέρωται to be on the subsequent revelations through the preached gospel rather than on the initial manifestation). He concludes his paragraph by saying that 'emphasis upon the faith of believers at this stage in Paul's argument seems unlikely for a number of reasons' (p. 74).

But p. 75 shows that he has massively misunderstood some, at any rate, of the scholars he criticizes. He argues that Paul would not be likely to 'maintain that the revelation of God's righteousness was dependent upon or mediated by the faith of believers on hearing the gospel', and goes on to list a series of objections to the objective genitive interpretation:

(i) it 'detracts . . . from the sufficiency of God's grace manifested in Christ';

(ii) it 'contradicts Paul's previous assessment of humanity's
unwillingness to respond to God';

(iii) it 'fails to accommodate the "pastness" of the initial
revelation of God's righteousness attested in 3.21';

(iv) it makes Paul guilty of 'unnecessary redundancy in style',
'given that εἰς πάντας τοὺς πιστεύοντας relates to
human faith in Jesus Christ'; and

(v) it 'places the emphasis in the disclosure of God's righteousness upon human response rather than divine initiative'.

These would be weighty charges, if they were true.

But to take the personal genitive in διὰ πίστεως Ἰησοῦ
Χριστοῦ as objective does not mean that one is suggesting that the
human response 'qualifies' the revelation of God's righteousness
or that that revelation is 'dependent upon or mediated by' the faith
of those who hear. The structure of the sentence clearly associates
the phrase not with πεφανέρωται but with δικαιοσύνη. It is
added surely in order to indicate that the only appropriate response
to God's δικαιοσύνη is simply to accept it as his altogether
undeserved gift given in Jesus Christ. It does not make the
revelation of God's righteousness in the on-going preaching of the
gospel dependent on that response; still less is there any question
of its making the revelation of that righteousness in the gospel
events themselves in any way so dependent. In reply to Wallis's
several objections:

(i) To indicate what is the appropriate human response to
God's gracious action in no way detracts from the
sufficiency of God's grace. To recognize that it makes
possible, and calls forth, a response on the part of human
beings does not call its sufficiency in question.

(ii) The reference to human faith in no way contradicts what
Paul has said of men's unresponsiveness to God; for faith,
as Paul understands it, 'is not a qualification which some
men already possess in themselves so that the gospel, when
it comes to them, finds them eligible to receive its benefits

... [it] is the openness to the gospel which God Himself creates'.[7]

(iii) The 'pastness' of 'the gospel events in their objectiveness as events which took place at a particular time in the past and are quite independent of, and distinct from, the response of men to them' is surely in no way called in question by recognizing that, when those events are recalled in the preaching, the appropriate response of the hearers is faith in Jesus Christ.

(iv) Dunn's answer to this objection, as raised earlier by R. B. Hays and M. D. Hooker, is surely adequate. εἰς πάντας τοὺς πιστεύοντας is required 'in order to emphasize the πάντας ... Students of Romans will not need to be reminded that this "all" is a thematic word in the letter, being used again and again, often with varying degrees of redundancy ... (see particularly 1.5, 16; 2.10; 4.11, 16; 10.4, 11–13). The usage in 3.22 is simply part of a sustained motif.'[8]

(v) The assertion that the double reference to human faith in v. 22 (if Ἰησοῦ Χριστοῦ is understood as objective) places the emphasis upon human response rather than on the divine initiative is plausible only on the assumption that faith in Christ is what a good many commentators on Romans have been at pains to explain that it is not.

On p. 76 Wallis interrupts his discussion of Romans 3.21–26, in order to try to build up a case for understanding Paul's thought to be that 'the righteousness and, particularly, its initial revelation is mediated by Jesus Christ's πίστις'. He claims that in the Old Testament God's righteousness and God's faithfulness are often synonymous. So we should ask what is the relationship between God's faithfulness and Christ's πίστις. He finds the idea that God's faithfulness can find expression through a human being in Psalm 89, and a further development of the idea in the Psalms of

---

[7] C. E. B. Cranfield, *A Critical and Exegetical Commentary on the Epistle to the Romans* 1, Edinburgh, [7]1990, p. 90.

[8] Dunn, op. cit., pp. 740–1.

Solomon. This background, he claims, provides 'a context in which Paul's διὰ πίστεως Ἰησοῦ Χριστοῦ in Romans 3.22 can be interpreted meaningfully as a subjective genitive, referring to the πίστις of Jesus Christ, the messiah, through which the covenantal faithfulness or righteousness of God is revealed' (p. 78). He then turns to Paul's quotation of Habakkuk in Romans 1.17, and, taking ἐκ πίστεως not with ὁ δίκαιος but with the verb ζήσεται, argues that, for Paul, ὁ δίκαιος 'refers primarily to Christ who lived by faith' (p. 81), and that the purport of ἐκ πίστεως εἰς πίστιν in v. 17a may well be that Jesus's 'life of faith (ἐκ πίστεως) provides the basis for the righteousness and faith (εἰς πίστιν) of all people' (p. 82).

But have we not here a very wilful exegesis? Could Paul have expected those who heard his letter read to realize that they were to understand the quotation as referring to Christ, when he had not mentioned Christ since vv. 8 and 9, but had clearly referred to the Christian believer in v. 16? And the modern exegete must surely take into consideration the formulation of 5.1 (Δικαιωθέντες οὖν ἐκ πίστεως . . .), which undoubtedly refers to Christian believers, and makes Wallis's contention (p. 80) that Paul would not be likely to refer to the believer as 'righteous' highly questionable (cf. the use of δίκαιοι in 5.19). And I think that Wallis's claim (in arguing against connecting ἐκ πίστεως with ὁ δίκαιος) that appropriation of justification by believing in Christ and appropriation of justification by responding to God's revelation of his law by a life of covenantal faithfulness are in fact much the same sort of thing, and that it would be more in keeping with Paul's thought to see the significant contrast as being between justification on the basis of human response and justification on the basis of God's universal grace in Christ than between 'works' and 'faith', must surely be rejected.

With regard to v. 25 Wallis argues, against taking διὰ [τῆς] πίστεως to refer to believers' faith, that 'it seems theologically incoherent for Paul to maintain that the efficacy of Christ's sacrificial death is dependent upon human faith' (pp. 82–3). It would indeed be, if that were what Paul is doing! But, on the assumption that πίστεως refers to believers' faith, we may surely take him to mean not that God purposed[9] that Christ should be through men's faith a ἱλαστήριον by the shedding of his blood, but that God purposed that he should be a ἱλαστήριον by the shedding of his blood, the appropriate response to which on men's part would be faith. I think we may explain the awkward placing of διὰ [τῆς] πίστεως between ἱλαστήριον and ἐν τῷ αὐτοῦ αἵματι, which are surely meant to be connected together, as being due to Paul's recognition that to have placed it after ἐν τῷ αὐτοῦ αἵματι would have obscured the fact that the following εἰς ἔνδειξιν κ.τ.λ. must be connected with ὃν προέθετο ὁ θεὸς ἱλαστήριον ἐν τῷ αὐτοῦ αἵματι, and not with the phrase indicating the proper response of human beings to God's act in Christ. I take it that Paul inserted διὰ [τῆς] πίστεως, in spite of the serious damage this would do to his sentence, because he recognized the importance of insisting both that this ἱλαστήριον would demand a response of faith on the part of human beings and also that only faith could be an appropriate response, all thoughts of being able to establish a claim on God by our works being excluded.

Wallis thinks that διὰ [τῆς] πίστεως should be understood as referring to Jesus' faith. But in what sense was Christ to be ἱλαστήριον 'through his faith'? I do not think that the references to faith in the passages concerning Jewish martyrs in 4 Maccabees 16.18–23; also 5.25; 7.19, 21; 15.24; 17.2, and 1 Maccabees 2.59, and the evidence of the close relationship between faith and obedience in Paul, are enough to give credibility to Wallis' case. It may well be true that Jesus in his earthly life was a man of faith and that he retained his faith to the very end; but I fail to see how his faith was that which made his dying efficacious for the atonement of human beings' sins, which διὰ [τῆς] πίστεως (if the reference is to Jesus' faith) would surely mean that it was. Wallis's question on p. 85, 'But does the verse explain how Christ's death acts as an ἱλαστήριον for God?' and his observation that 'ἐν τῷ αὐτοῦ αἵματι can be taken as an instrumental dative of price with the sense that atonement is achieved through his [i.e. Christ's] faith at

---

[9] Wallis, p. 72, translates προέθετο by 'put forward'. For reasons for pre-ferring 'purposed' see Cranfield, op. cit., pp. 208–10.

the cost of his blood' suggest that he is thinking of the ἱλαστήριον as an action of Christ by which he somehow satisfies God. But did Paul really think in this way? Did he not see God's action and Christ's action as a unity and the ἱλαστήριον as something accomplished by God in Christ?[10] Is this not why he can say that God proves his love for us by the fact that Christ died for us (Rom. 5.8) and can use 'the love of Christ' (8.35) and 'the love of God which is in Christ Jesus our Lord' (8.39) as synonyms? If Paul thought that God's very self was present in the Son who suffered, would he think in terms of Christ's faith making his death act as a ἱλαστήριον for God?

On p. 87 Wallis turns to the consideration of τὸν ἐκ πίστεως Ἰησοῦ in v. 26. He first makes the point that here Paul uses the simple name Jesus without the addition of 'Christ' or 'Lord', and claims that where he does this, 'the focus tends to be upon the earthly existence of Jesus' (p. 88). But this cannot be accepted as a reason for taking this genitive as subjective, since it is clearly not a rule that bound Paul. In 2 Corinthians 4.5, for example, Ἰησοῦν Χριστόν is immediately followed by Ἰησοῦν without any obvious change of significance (cf. the other occurrences of the simple name in this chapter, especially in v. 14; also 1 Thess. 1.10; 4.14).

Wallis translates the phrase: 'the one [who lives] from Jesus' faith [*or* the one participating in Jesus' faith]' (p. 72). But, if that is the meaning of the phrase in 3.26, must we not say that this contradicts the πάντας τοὺς πιστεύοντας of v. 22? If God's justification, is only for those who live from Jesus' faith or actually participate in it, is this not justification by works with a vengeance? For to say that someone 'lives from Jesus' faith' or participates in Jesus' faith is surely to say much more than to say that someone believes in, trusts, Jesus Christ. Such an interpretation is surprising, coming from one who has only a few pages earlier criticized those who accept the objective genitive explanation of πίστις Χριστοῦ for putting too much emphasis on the human response.

[10] Cf. Cranfield, op. cit., p. 217; also 2, p. 840.

As to Wallis' argument from τῷ ἐκ πίστεως 'Αβραάμ in 4.16, it is true that both this phrase and the one we are concerned with exhibit the construction ὁ ἐκ πίστεως plus a genitive, but the fact that in 4.16 the following genitive is subjective does not necessarily mean that the following genitive here must also be subjective (these are the only places in the Pauline epistles or indeed in the New Testament where this construction appears). In the absence of any conclusive evidence that Paul avoided using πίστις with an objective genitive, it is surely just as reasonable to argue from the fact that there are a number of places where ἐκ πίστεως occurs in close association with δικαιοῦν, δίκαιος or δικαιοσύνη, and clearly denotes the believer's faith (e.g. 3.30; 5.1; 9.30, 32; Gal. 3.8; 5.5), that it is probable that πίστις here too refers to the believer's faith.

The last part of Wallis' discussion of the Romans evidence is headed 'Human faith in the dispensation of faith-grace' (pp. 98–102). I found it very hard to follow. I cannot help wondering whether the author, if the work of the Holy Spirit had had a larger place in his thinking, might not have had less difficulty with the emphasis which he feels the exponents of the objective genitive explanation put on the human response. I doubt very much whether Paul would have been happy with the conclusion that in Romans 8 'Paul is not making a temporal distinction between pre- and post-conversion situations, but establishing an existential one in which each person either gives God permission to work through his Spirit or relies on his own resources' (p. 102). And the final sentence of this section, 'Life in the Spirit is certainly about coming within the influence of the Spirit of Christ, but each prompting of the Spirit must be recognized and, so to, speak, given permission before the individual participates in the realities secured in the death and resurrection of Jesus', seems to me equally unsatisfactory as an exposition of Pauline teaching. Would it not be truer to Pauline teaching to say that it is the Holy Spirit who in the first place makes a human being free to believe and who thereafter renews and sustains the faith he has created?

Wallis then turns to the relevant Galatians passages (p. 102). He argues that, if πίστεως in its two occurrences in Galatians 2.16

as well as ἐπιστεύσαμεν refers to the faith of believers, 'the emphasis within this key verse for Paul's soteriology falls rather awkwardly upon the believer rather than Christ' (p. 105). But this opinion would seem to be based on the assumption that faith in Christ, as understood by Paul, is something very different from what a great many students of Paul have understood it to be. For Paul, as we understand him, it is most certainly not on the believer that the emphasis falls, when he speaks of faith in Christ, nor on the believer's faith, but on the object of faith, Christ himself. Wallis' questions on p. 106, 'Upon what, then, does Paul encourage the Galatian Christians to base their standing before God? Belief in Christ or works of the law? Or the more fundamental reality of the faith of Christ himself . . . ?' imply that those who take the genitives Ἰησοῦ Χριστοῦ and Χριστοῦ in Galatians 2.16 as objective are suggesting that Paul was encouraging the Galatian Christians to see their faith as the basis of their standing before God. But that is altogether untrue. Christians are not to put their trust in their own faith, in themselves as believing, but, abandoning all self-trust, to put all their trust in Christ. It seems to me that Wallis has thoroughly misunderstood the views of those whom he is criticizing, having assumed that they must share that horrible distortion of evangelical teaching which makes faith into a human meritorious work, a distortion which admittedly is to be found in some circles, but which it is quite unfair to attribute to all those who accept the objective genitive explanation of the πίστις Χριστοῦ passages.

With regard to 2.19b–20, Wallis comments: 'Paul's . . . life is now enabled by the faith of the son of God, whose love for him was epitomized in sacrificial death. Further, given the intimacy of the language (ζῶ δὲ οὐκέτι ἐγώ, ζῇ δὲ ἐν ἐμοὶ Χριστός), it would be difficult to envisage how Paul's response of faith could be meaningfully distinguished from that of the son of God who dwells within him' (p. 116). And in a footnote he adds: 'It is also worth noting that even if Gal. 2.20 does refer to faith in the son of God, it is still Christ who dwells within Paul. Who, then, is the Paul – separate from the "Christ within" – who so believes?' But, when the conclusion is reached that it is difficult to see a meaningful distinction between the faith of the Christian and Christ's own faith, has not the notion of participation in Christ been taken too far? And, when the author later on speaks of 'an existential continuity between Christ's faith and the faith of believers' (p. 125), must we not ask whether the fact that, while he was sinless, we are all manifestly sinners does not constitute a serious interruption of that continuity? The faith that can meaningfully be ascribed to one who was truly obedient to God is surely something very different from the faith of those who have to live by God's forgiveness every moment. Paul's language in Galatians 2.19b–20 is certainly bold and has proved liable to be misunderstood; but so long as τοῦ υἱοῦ τοῦ θεοῦ is taken as an objective genitive, there is a safeguard present to maintain the distinction between Christ and his apostle unblurred. When, however, the genitive is understood as subjective that safeguard is removed.

The last πίστις Χριστοῦ verse in Galatians is 3.22, which Wallis translates: 'But the scripture has imprisoned all things under [the power of] sin, so that the promise on the basis of Jesus Christ's faith might be given to those who believe [or who participate in the dispensation of faith]' (p. 103). The order of the English words suggests that 'on the basis of Jesus Christ's faith' is meant to be connected with 'the promise'; but Paul, had he meant this, would probably have written either ἡ ἐκ πίστεως Ἰησοῦ Χριστοῦ ἐπαγγελία or ἡ ἐπαγγελία ἡ ἐκ πίστεως Ἰησοῦ Χριστοῦ.[11] But more probably the words should be connected with the verb 'might be given'. Once more the author confidently accepts the subjective genitive explanation. On p. 117 he makes the following assertions: 'for Paul, the promise is not simply appropriated by faith (τοῖς πιστεύουσιν, 3.22), but by partici-pating – through faith – in Jesus Christ, who inherited the promise through faith (ἐκ πίστεως Ἰησοῦ Χριστοῦ). In consequence, the faith of believers can never be dissociated from the faith of Christ. It is his faith which makes the faith of others possible and enables

[11] The case of ὁ δὲ δίκαιος ἐκ πίστεως ζήσεται in 1.17 is rather different, since Paul might well not want to change the word-order of the Habakkuk quotation.

them to participate in its inheritance.' But the basis in the text of Galatians for these assertions seems altogether too questionable for them to be accepted. If the faith of Jesus Christ was as central to Paul's thought as these assertions indicate, it is strange indeed that his letters contain no single unambiguous reference to it. Once again I think we can say that the objective genitive explanation is by far the more probable.

The last of the seven πίστις Χριστοῦ verses is Philippians 3.9, and here too Wallis argues for the subjective genitive. He translates: 'and be found in him, not having a righteousness of my own which comes from the law, but a righteousness from God through [or by means of] Christ's faith which leads to [or for the purpose of] faith' (p. 118). Wallis notes that there is a contrast between two things: 'righteousness ἐκ νόμου appropriated by human effort' and 'righteousness ἐκ θεοῦ appropriated διὰ πίστεως Ἰησοῦ' (p. 119). He then argues that, if διὰ πίστεως Χριστοῦ is understood as 'by faith in Christ', the two contrasted things 'become remarkably similar in their emphasis upon human response'; that 'this hardly reflects the centrality of Christ for Paul'; and that it 'rests upon a dichotomy between "works of the law" and "faith in Christ" not evident in Philippians' (p. 120). But the first and second of these objections rest on a misunderstanding of what faith in Christ is. In faith in Christ the emphasis is not on the subject but altogether on the object, and the human response is itself God-given. The centrality of Christ is in no way called in question. In reply to the third objection, it may be pointed out that the paragraph 3.2–11 is the only part of Philippians where the subject-matter dealt with was likely to occasion this dichotomy.

Wallis suggests that Paul thinks of each Christian's relationship to God as being 'grounded in a right-relatedness to God communicated through the faith of Christ', and that 'the link between chapter 3 and the Christ-hymn of Philippians 2.6–11 . . . and the relationship between obedience and faith in the apostle's thinking . . . , together with the flow of the letter, would encourage Paul's readers to interpret the establishing of God's righteousness διὰ πίστεως Χριστοῦ in terms of his obedient self-giving in death mentioned in chapter 2' (pp. 120–1). But I find it very difficult to take this seriously as exegesis of what we actually have in the text.

Wallis finally explains ἐπὶ τῇ πίστει as meaning: 'which leads to [*or* for the purpose of] faith [of believers]', attributing a final force to ἐπί, as in Galatians 5.13 and 1 Thessalonians 4.7. But in those two examples the nouns are without the definite article. Dunn is surely right in saying that the presence of the definite article here 'must mean that Paul was referring to the same faith both times – "the faith", that is, the faith just mentioned'.[12] This grammatical point surely excludes the possibility of taking the first πίστις in the verse to refer to Christ's, and the second to believers', faith. I think we can only conclude that πίστις Χριστοῦ here must mean 'faith in Christ'.

In his concluding remarks on Paul Wallis claims to 'have discovered substantial grounds for maintaining that in each case [that is, in each of the seven πίστις Χριστοῦ constructions] Paul had Christ's own faith in mind', and also lists in a footnote other occurrences of πίστις in Paul's letters which he thinks may refer to Christ's faith: e.g. Romans 1.17 (Hab. 2.4); 3.25; Galatians 3.2, 5, 11 (Hab. 2.4), 14, 23–26; Philippians 1.27 (p. 124, and n. 250).

In conclusion, I want to make a number of points.

(i) In view of the large number of times that πιστεύειν and πίστις occur in the New Testament and in the Pauline epistles in particular, it seems to me that the statistical evidence which I summarized above should carry great weight. The absence of any clear statement that Jesus 'believed', 'had faith' (πιστεύειν) and of any unambiguous use of πίστις of Christ's own faith, and the fact that there are quite unambiguous references to faith in Christ are surely persuasive arguments against the subjective genitive interpretation and for the objective.

(ii) When we add to the statistical evidence just mentioned the grammatical evidence adduced by Hultgren and others, showing that, apart from the seven occurrences of the formulation which are under discussion (in all of which it

[12] Dunn, op. cit., p. 744.

is anarthrous), πίστις is almost, if not quite, invariably preceded by the definite article whenever the following genitive is clearly to be understood as subjective, the case against the subjective genitive explanation seems to me to be already so strong that we should contemplate setting it aside only if there are overwhelmingly convincing exegetical reasons for so doing.

(iii) None of the exegetical arguments of which I am aware that have been put forward in support of taking πίστις in these places as referring to Christ's own faith seems to me convincing, and like, Dunn,[13] I am puzzled by the fact that so many able scholars are seeking with such enthusiasm to promote this interpretation.

(iv) It is well known that Paul uses πίστις to denote several different things. At any rate these may be distinguished: (a) faithfulness, trustworthiness (e.g. Rom. 3.5, of God; Gal. 5.22, of believers); (b) a special charisma given only to some believers (e.g. 1 Cor. 12.8–11); (c) faith in the sense of *fides qua creditur*; (d) faith in the sense of confidence that one's faith in sense (c) allows one to do or not do certain things (e.g. Rom. 14.1, 2 (the verb), 22, 23). Whether a further meaning, (e) faith in the sense of *fides quae creditur*, the body of doctrine believed, is already to be seen in Paul is disputed. Of these I think we can take (c) as the characteristic Pauline sense. But the view that Paul referred to the faith of Jesus Christ (πίστις sense (c)) seems to me to be open to an objection which has not been given the attention it deserves. I get the impression that 'faith' (both πίστις and πιστεύειν) in its most characteristic Pauline use carries with it what may be called a 'negative' or 'excluding' or indeed a 'sinfulness-admitting' sense. To be justified ἐκ πίστεως is to receive as God's free, utterly undeserved gift in Jesus Christ a status of righteousness before him. ἐκ πίστεως excludes all thought of earning that status by anything one can do. So there is a contrast

[13] Op. cit., p. 744.

between justification ἐκ πίστεως and justification ἐξ ἔργων. Faith then excludes everything by which one might think to establish for oneself a claim on God, to put him under an obligation. To believe in Christ Jesus (e.g. εἰς Χριστὸν Ἰησοῦν πιστεύειν in Gal. 2.16) is to put all one's trust in God's grace in him, to the exclusion of all self-trust and all attempts to justify oneself. It is the attitude of one who knows and confesses that he is a sinner. This 'negative' function of πίστις/πιστεύειν is very evident in Paul's appeal to Abraham in Romans 4. Whatever Paul's Jewish contemporaries thought about Abraham's faith, it is apparent that, although he recognized that from a human point of view there was indeed something heroic about Abraham's believing God's promise when all his circumstances contradicted it (vv. 17b–21), Paul nevertheless understood Abraham's faith as the faith of one who, having no meritorious works of his own to his credit, can only trust in the God who justifies the ungodly (τὸν δικαιοῦντα τὸν ἀσεβῆ), the implication surely being that Abraham too is ungodly like all the rest of fallen humanity. And the point already made in vv. 1–5 is further driven home by vv. 6–8, in which LXX Psalm 31.1–2 is brought in to help to interpret Genesis 15.6, the basic biblical text concerning Abraham's faith: 'even as David also pronounces the blessing of the man to whom God reckons righteousness apart from works: "Blessed are those whose iniquities have been forgiven and whose sins have been covered; blessed is the man whose sin the Lord will in no wise reckon"'.

If πίστις, when used in what I have called above 'sense (c)', was in Paul's mind as strongly associated with the situation of the sinner who knows that he has no ground on which to stand before God except God's own sheer grace in Jesus Christ as I think it was, then this would suggest that it would not be likely to come at all naturally to him to speak of Jesus Christ's πίστις. It would also suggest that we should be wise to hesitate about trying to construct a theology in which Jesus Christ's faith has an important place.

8

Giving a Dog a Bad Name

A note on H. Räisänen's Paul and the Law

Heikki Räisänen's *Paul and the Law*, Tübingen, 1983, has been warmly welcomed.[1] There is no doubt that it is a significant contribution to Pauline studies, and we are indebted to its author for having stated his views so forcefully and unambiguously. He has made some useful points, and the provocativeness of his book will surely stimulate his readers to further reflection and research. But 'Has he been fair to St Paul?' is a question needing to be asked.

Let me say at once that I have no intention of claiming that Paul's letters are free from inconsistencies. Like all other fallen human beings Paul was no doubt liable to err and to be inconsistent. But that his epistles are as riddled with self-contradictions as Räisänen would have us believe I find hard to accept. Liberally scattered throughout his book are such judgments as these: 'Apparently without noticing it, Paul is thus tacitly operating with a double concept of "law"' (p. 21); 'Of course Paul is quite capable of turning verses of the OT into their opposites' (p. 95, n. 13); 'these inadvertent admissions' (p. 107); 'irreconcilable tension' (p. 110); 'one more blatant self-contradiction' (p. 153, n. 120); 'As so often, his theology has a Janus face. He points in one (covenantal) direction and goes in another (without, I think, realizing where he actually is)' (p. 188); 'identifying in an unreflective way the

* First published in *Journal for the Study of the New Testament* 38 (1990), pp. 77-85.

---

[1] See, for example, A. J. M. Wedderburn's review article in *SJT* 38 (1985), pp. 613–22.

Septuagintal πίστις, with his own "faith"' (p. 189, n. 130); 'apparently without realizing the looseness of his speech' (p. 199); 'This assertion is demonstrated by exaggerating blanket accusations' (p. 199); 'In sum, I am not able to find in the relevant literature [that is, in the rest of the NT and in the other early Christian writings which he considers] *any* conception of the law which involves such inconsistencies or such arbitrariness as does Paul's' (p. 228). Was Paul really quite as inconsistent, confused and incompetent, quite as careless and unreflective, as this? As I read Räisänen's book, I could not help thinking that for him Paul just cannot do right. It seemed to be a case of 'Give a dog a bad name, and hang him.'

A definitive answer to the question whether Räisänen has been fair to Paul could only be given on the basis of a full and careful examination of the detailed exegesis contained in his book. In a short article it is impossible to examine all this material. We shall concentrate on just one of his chapters – chapter III, which is entitled 'Can the law be fulfilled?' If in this limited sample it appears that he has been unfair, readers will surely be well advised to exercise caution with regard to the rest. My own copy of the book certainly contains a good many question marks pencilled in the margins in the other chapters as well as in the one I have chosen for special scrutiny here.

In the brief first section (pp. 94–6), which has the heading 'Fulfilling the whole law is impossible', the author appeals particularly to Galatians 3.10–12 and 5.3 as proving that it was Paul's view that the law requires 'total obedience' and that such total obedience is impossible (p. 95). With regard to this section we need not, I think, quarrel with the author, even though there were one or two places in it which gave rise to a little uneasiness.

In section 2, which is headed 'All are under sin', Räisänen deals with Romans 1.18–3.20. In the concluding paragraph of the section he quotes with approval S. Sandmel's description of Paul's account as 'grotesque and vicious' and his opinion that a Jewish reader 'must . . . conclude . . . that Paul lacks for those who disagree with him the love which he described in 1 Cor. 13', adding his own comment: 'A Christian reader should agree!' Räisänen's concluding judgment is that 'Paul's argument is here simply a piece of propagandist denigration' (p. 101).

In reply to this it must be said that, if Paul really were simply pronouncing his own judgment on Gentiles and Jews, then Räisänen's condemnation of him would indeed be largely justified. As an historian's assessment of the moral condition of his contemporaries Romans 1.18–3.20 would indeed be grossly unfair. But, in view of the surely undeniable parallelism between ἀποκαλύπτεται γὰρ ὀργὴ θεοῦ in 1.18 and δικαιοσύνη γὰρ θεοῦ ἐν αὐτῷ [that is, in the preaching of the gospel] ἀποκαλύπτεται in 1.17, we must, surely, understand Romans 1.18–3.20 as being, in Paul's intention, not his own moral evaluation of his contemporaries but his witness to the gospel's judgment of all human beings, that judgment which the gospel itself pronounces and which can be recognized and submitted to only in the light of the gospel, that judgment which Paul has heard and to which he has himself already submitted.[2] It seems to us that Räisänen has radically misunderstood this passage, because he has considered it in detachment from its context and in particular from what immediately precedes it, and so, instead of recognizing in it Paul's witness to the judgment, which (having been once for all manifested in the gospel events) is now being again and again revealed whenever the gospel is preached, has seen merely a moralistic attempt on Paul's part to demonstrate by empirical arguments the sinfulness of non-Christian Gentiles and Jews.

Räisänen seems to see Christians as being outside the scope of this passage. It is presumably because he does so that he can complain that 'Paul has double standards when evaluating Jewish and Christian transgressions respectively' (p. 100). But, when this passage is considered in its context, it is surely clear that its purpose is to establish that all human beings (Jesus Christ alone excepted) 'are under sin'. Christians are surely embraced in the ἄνθρωποι of 1.18, the Ἰουδαῖοί τε καὶ Ἕλληνες πάντες of

---

[2] It is true that in 3.9 Paul used the word προῃτιασάμεθα (RV: 'we before laid to the charge . . . of'); but this surely should not be pressed to mean that he was thinking of himself as the originator of the charge, rather than as the witness to the judgment which the cross has disclosed.

3.9 and the πάντες of 3.23 (though it is, of course, true that Paul will have more to say about them than just that they are included in this judgment). We take it that Paul's basic witness to the gospel's judgment of human beings is in 1.18–32, and that these verses are the disclosure not only of the idolatry of ancient and modern paganism but also of the idolatry cherished in Israel, in the Christian church and in the thoughts and life of each Christian believer. The Jews are then specially dealt with in what follows, not out of any anti-Jewish prejudice but because Paul recognizes that they do indeed have a real moral superiority. It is surely precisely because he recognizes this superiority that he is concerned to show that even this undoubted superiority does not make them an exception to the general judgment indicated in 1.18–32. It seems to us that in this section, far from substantiating his accusations against Paul's fairness, Räisänen has shown himself to be seriously confused in his understanding of Paul's argument.

In section 3 ('Non-Christians fulfilling the law') Räisänen discusses Romans 2.14–15 and 26–27. He sees them as standing 'in flat contradiction to the main thesis' of 1.18–3.20 that all are under sin (p. 103). On pp. 103–5 he summarizes several suggested explanations of these verses which have been put forward with a view to reconciling them with Paul's main concern in 1.18–3.20, but concludes that none of them is credible. We therefore, he thinks, 'have to accept that Paul is really speaking of Gentiles who fulfil the law outside the Christian community' (p. 105). He goes on to stress that Paul is here not interested in the Gentiles for their own sake but is merely using them 'as convenient weapons to hit the Jew with' (p. 106) and to maintain that, when Paul is thinking of Gentiles in this incidental way and not actually reflecting on their situation, it comes quite naturally to him to think that they can fulfil the law (p. 106). He also suggests that we should conclude that, when Paul is not actually reflecting on the situation of the Jews, he can think of them too as fulfilling the law (he appeals to Phil. 3.6 in support). So he comes to the position: 'The theological thesis in Rom. 1.18–3.20 is that all are under sin and that, therefore, no one can fulfil the law. Inadvertently, however, Paul admits even within that very section that, on another level of his consciousness at least, he does not share this idea. Paul's mind is divided' (pp. 106f). Clearly then, for Räisänen, there is at this point 'a formidable tension in Paul's thought' (p. 107).

But is this fair? Even on the assumption that Paul must be 'speaking of Gentiles who fulfil the law outside the Christian community', it is doubtful whether he was quite as confused as Räisänen has made out. And, if the explanation that Paul was thinking of the Gentile Christians (an explanation going back to patristic times and accepted by a number of recent interpreters, though dismissed as incredible by Räisänen) is right, as we are still confident that it is,[3] an intelligible line of thought can be discerned.

---

[3] I tried to discuss the matter in *A Critical and Exegetical Commentary on the Epistle to the Romans* 1, Edinburgh, ⁶1987, pp. 151–63, 172–4. Räisänen's five reasons for rejecting this explanation (pp. 104–5) do not seem to me at all convincing. In reply to the first (that 'In this context it is very difficult to take ἔθνη in any other sense than "non-Jew" in general') it may be said that there is no question of taking the word in any other sense than 'Gentiles' or 'non-Jews'. What is being suggested is that, when Paul used ἔθνη, which here, on Räisänen's own interpretation just as much as on the Gentile Christian interpretation, must mean not 'the Gentiles' (in the sense of 'the Gentiles as a whole or all Gentiles') but 'Gentiles' (in the sense of 'some Gentiles' – cf. the similarly inarticulate ἔθνη in 9.30), he was thinking of the Christian ones. The context does not seem to present any difficulty for this. Both Räisänen's second and third objections (that 'it is inconceivable that Paul could say that Gentile Christians fulfil the law *by nature* . . . for the Christians' fulfilment of the law is the fruit of the *Spirit*, and 'how could he say that Gentile Christians are without the law in the sense that it is unknown to them?') fail, if it is accepted that φύσει in v. 14 should be connected with ἔχοντα rather than with ποιῶσιν. His fourth objection (that ἑαυτοῖς εἰσιν νόμος is a surprising thing for Paul to say of Gentile Christians) does not seem at all strong. Why should not Paul have made use of this stereotyped expression to indicate that these Gentile Christians inwardly desire to obey the law? With the fifth objection (that it is unlikely that an allusion to Jeremiah 31.33 was intended in v. 15) we are in danger of falling into a circular argument, since the main reason for denying that Jeremiah 31.33 is alluded to here is the assumption that what is referred to in Romans 2.15 is a non-eschatological fact of Gentile life, while Jeremiah 31.33 refers to an eschatological work of God to be effected on Israel; but, if Romans 2.15 refers to Gentile Christians, this objection would fail, since Paul clearly did think that God's eschatological promises were beginning to be fulfilled in the life of the Christian community, both Jewish and Gentile.

In the course of his attempt to show that the Jews are no exception to the judgment which 1.18–32 attests, he stresses the importance of deeds (ἔργα in v. 6, ἔργου in v. 7, κατεργαζομένου in v. 9, ἐργαζομένῳ in v. 10, ποιηταί in v. 13, ποιῶσιν in v. 14). It is not hearing the law but doing it which is decisive. The point Paul is concerned to make in all this is the negative one, that the Jews are not an exception to the judgment which the gospel unveils; but, in making this point, he also alludes – in anticipation of what he will have to say later on – to those works of the Christian believer, which, while they in no way establish any claim on God, are nevertheless, as a sign of faith and gratitude, a token movement in the direction of obedience, well-pleasing to God. If this interpretation of 2.14f and 26f is accepted, there is no 'flat contradiction' between these verses and the main thesis of 1.18–3.20.

Section 4, which has the heading, 'Non-Christians cannot do good at all', begins with the surprising claim: 'It is hardly necessary to argue once more that the famous passage Romans 7.14–25 is not intended by Paul as a description of the Christian. It can by now be taken for granted that he is speaking of man's existence under the law' (p. 109). But, in view of the scale and the intensity of the still continuing debate over the interpretation of these verses, it is surely quite intolerable for Räisänen to suggest that the matter is just about settled and that the interpretation which he favours can now be taken for granted. If this interpretation is rejected, as we think it should be, and the view that Paul is describing the life of the Christian is accepted, then Räisänen's appeal to Romans 7.14–25 in this section is quite inapposite. Unfortunately, he confines his case in this section almost entirely to this passage; only in the last paragraph does he also appeal to the evidence of Romans 8.4–11. A reference to Romans 8.5–11 was certainly apposite here. But a serious attempt to draw out Paul's meaning in these verses, and particularly in v. 8, was surely called for. It does not seem to us to have been made.

In section 5, which is headed 'Christians fulfil the law', Räisänen claims that 'Paul assumes within the framework of his theological theory . . . that the Christians fulfil what is required by the law', and appeals to Galatians 5.14ff; Romans 13.8–10; Romans 8.4 in support of this (p. 113). Here, Räisänen explains, 'law' is understood in terms of the moral content of the law (pp. 113f). He sees Romans 8.4, 9–11; 6.14a; Galatians 5.16, 23b as expressing Paul's optimistic view of Christians (pp. 114f), a view which Räisänen insists on understanding as being thoroughly naïve. He speaks of Paul's 'extravagant statement' (p. 114, n. 103), his 'optimistic assertions' (p. 116), his being 'not conscious of any personal sin in his own life' (p. 118), and suggests that 'The notion of the shortness of time, the eschatological fervour, made it seem a real possibility that the congregations might be able to live a sinless life for the short time still left before the parousia' (p. 118). At the same time Räisänen sees hints of reality in such passages as 1 Corinthians 5.1–5, 9–13; 6.1–20; 2 Corinthians 12.20f; Galatians 5.15; 6.1, which refer to the existence of sin within the Christian communities. But he does not at all allow for the possibility that the evidence that Paul was aware of continuing sin in the church ought to make us ask whether perhaps Paul's own meaning in those other passages, which Räisänen assumes express a doctrinaire optimistic view of the life of Christians, may not actually have been very much less naïve than he thinks. He asserts that the 'concession to reality' in 1 Corinthians 3.3 'flatly contradicts the black-and-white distinction between those in the flesh and those in the Spirit made in Rom. 8.5ff' (p. 116). But may the truth not be that Romans 8.5ff was never meant by Paul as the simplistic contrast between Christians and non-Christians which Räisänen apparently assumes that it must have been?

Räisänen concludes this section by quoting, apparently with full approval, Wernle's words: 'Paul does not want to see the problem of sin in Christian life; therefore it does not exist' (p. 118). The unfairness of this verdict is, surely, sufficiently clear from the presence of those passages which Räisänen recognizes as hints of reality. And for those, who, unlike him, take the view that Romans 7.14–25 refers to Christians, including the apostle himself at the time of the composition of Romans, the unfairness of the verdict is, of course, much more patently obvious – as also of the statement (quoted above) that Paul 'was not conscious of any personal sin in his own life'. Convinced as we are of the correctness of this view of Romans 7.14ff, we are also convinced that Romans 6, 7 and 8, taken together, as we cannot help thinking Paul meant them to be taken, present a properly balanced and thoroughly honest account of the sanctification of believers.

Sections 6 and 7 (headed 'Summary' and 'Analogies?' respectively need not detain us: the former is very slight (only sixteen lines), the latter a sort of appendix. By way of conclusion we make the following observations.

(i) While in several of Paul's letters a good deal is said concerning various aspects of the law, there is nowhere in the extant letters anything like an attempt to set out his understanding of it systematically as a whole. This means that the position of the scholar who wants to explain the structure of Paul's view of the law is a bit like that of a person who knows nothing about giraffes but has to try to draw a picture of one, having nothing to go on but someone's sketch of a giraffe, of which much of the central area has been obliterated. It is hardly surprising that it is difficult to understand how the various things which Paul has said about the law cohere together. Our best hope of being able to do so would seem to lie in having a personal rapport with the apostle's faith.

(ii) The fact that many of Paul's statements about the law belong to a context of controversy is a further difficulty. This has to be taken into account; and, since he had to fight on more than one front, we have to allow for considerable variation of emphasis according to the different opponents who claim his attention.

(iii) We get the impression that Räisänen's approach to his subject is very simplistic. His impatience with explanations which reckon with paradox or tension (p. 4) chimes with this. But theology is surely a field in which a hankering after simplistic solutions is particularly inappropriate. Here answers which are both simple and true are often not to be had.

(iv) That there is a variety of possible models of consistency should not be forgotten. Whether in considering the question of Paul's consistency or lack of it we have at the back of our minds a more or a less appropriate model may well be important. A field of wheat swept by a steady wind and a Guards' battalion reacting to a drill sergeant's orders would seem to be less suitable models of consistency for our purpose than a great work of architecture such as Durham Cathedral or the Royal Border Bridge. Neither Durham Cathedral nor the Royal Border Bridge could ever have been erected, let alone remained standing, had it not been for the careful balancing of contrary thrusts. No one in his senses would think of suggesting that a cathedral or a great bridge should be built on the principle of all thrusts in the same direction. Perhaps this should incline us to be cautious about writing off Paul's understanding of the law as hopelessly inconsistent ?

(v) It is, we believe, a consequence of his simplistic approach that Räisänen is unable to recognize the appropriateness of Paul's using terms expressive of the idea of fulfilment[4] both to denote the perfect obedience to the law, which no man other than Jesus has accomplished, and also to denote those beginnings of being turned in the direction of obedience for which the Holy Spirit sets the believer free, that response of gratitude to God's grace, which, though it falls far short of being perfect obedience and in no way establishes any human claim on God, is nevertheless, in spite of all its falterings and brokenness, something with which God in his goodness deigns to be well-pleased.

---

[4] τελεῖν, πληροῦν, φυλάσσειν, ποιεῖν, ποιητής, πράσσειν are used.

9

Has the Old Testament Law a Place in the Christian Life?

A response to Professor Westerholm

Stephen Westerholm's *Israel's Law and the Church's Faith: Paul and His Recent Interpreters*[1] has had an exceptionally enthusiastic welcome, and is undoubtedly a very important book. Not surprisingly it has already proved influential, and it seems likely that it will have a widespread influence for a good many years to come. Because this is so, it is specially desirable that its argumentation should be subjected to adequate scrutiny. The purpose of this essay is to examine just one chapter in detail, the one entitled 'The Law and Christian Behavior' (Chapter X). This chapter is selected for examination because the question, to which it seeks to give a definitive answer, namely, whether or not the Old Testament law has a place in the Christian life, is, I believe, a matter of vital importance for the health and integrity of the church.

I

Westerholm's contention is that Paul saw no continuing rôle for the law in the life of Christians. At the beginning of the chapter he argues that Paul would hardly have been charged with encouraging

---

* First published in *Irish Biblical Studies* 15 (1993), pp. 50–64.

[1] Grand Rapids, 1988.

sin, as Romans 3.8; 6.1, 15 imply that he was, had his position been simply either 'that the law's curse has been removed, though its precepts must be followed, or that the moral law stands, though the ritual law has been done away with' (p. 199). The fact that such a charge could be laid against him with some plausibility must mean, Westerholm suggests, that he went further than this and denied the Mosaic law any place in the Christian's life. But this argument lacks cogency. Paul's teaching on justification by faith would surely have been likely to be misunderstood as encouragement to sin, however much it was accompanied by exhortation to obey the commands of the law.

Westerholm goes on to try to establish five positions. The first is: 'That the ethical behavior which Paul expects of believers corresponds in content to the moral demands of the Mosaic code cannot be used to argue the abiding validity of the law'. With regard to this, it must, I think, be admitted that the overlap in content between Paul's moral teaching and the moral demands of the Mosaic law does not in itself prove that Paul regarded the law as still authoritative for Christians; but it is thoroughly consistent with the assumption that he did.

The second position which Westerholm seeks to establish is that 'Paul's statements that Christians "fulfill" the law are . . . an inadequate base for arguing that Christians are obligated to adhere to its precepts' (p. 199). He maintains that, when Paul speaks of Christians' fulfilling the law (he refers to Rom. 8.4; 13.8–10 and Gal. 5.14), he 'is describing, not prescribing, Christian behavior' (p. 201). According to Westerholm, what Paul is doing is not indicating the duty of Christians to try to fulfil the law, not setting before them an imperative, but making the claim that Christians do as a matter of fact fulfil the law. When he was describing 'a life lived in conformity with Christian principles', it was, 'for polemical reasons, important for him to say that Christian behavior is condemned by no law (Gal. 5.23), that the love which is the hallmark of Christian conduct in fact fulfills the law (Gal. 5.14; Rom. 13.8–10)' (pp. 201–2). On p. 219 Westerholm can actually speak of this claim which he thinks Paul is making as 'one-upmanship' on Paul's part.

But the ἵνα in Romans 8.4 is surely extremely significant. Paul is indicating that one purpose of God's saving deed in Christ was that the law's δικαίωμα (I take the word to mean here 'righteous requirement') might be fulfilled in us by our walking not according to the flesh but according to the Spirit. In v. 9a Paul uses the indicative. A process of sanctification is indeed going on in every Christian, but the διὰ ἁμαρτίαν in v. 10 would seem to imply that Christians are still sinners. We take it that the fulfilment spoken of in v. 4 is only begun, not something completed. That the implication of this passage is therefore that Christians must strive ever to move in the direction of the law's righteous requirement's being fulfilled in their lives seems to me clear enough.

In Romans 13.8–10 Paul speaks about the *debitum immortale*, the debt of love which we can never be finished with discharging. The point of v. 8b could be to state a reason for loving one another: to do so is to fulfil the law. More probably, I think, it is to be understood as explaining why the debt of love can never be fully discharged: it cannot be fully discharged, for, if there were people who really and truly and in the fullest sense loved their neighbours, they would have done what Paul in Romans 1.18–3.20 has shown to be altogether beyond the reach of Jews and Gentiles alike – they would have fulfilled the law. Paul goes on to indicate that the particular commandments of the 'second table' of the Decalogue are all summed up in the commandment of Leviticus 19.18, 'thou shalt love thy neighbour as thyself', and to state that love is the fulfilling of the law. But, since Paul was apparently well aware that Christians can very easily persuade themselves that they are loving when they are not (note that twice in his surviving letters he uses the word ἀνυπόκριτος with reference to love – in Romans 12.9 and 2 Corinthians 6.6), it seems most unlikely that he would have countenanced the idea that Christians should forget the particular commandments and rely on the commandment of love as a sufficient guide. Is it not more likely that he recognized that, while Christians certainly need the summary to save them from missing the wood for the trees and from understanding the particular commandments in a rigid, literalistic, unimaginative or loveless way,

111

they also need the particular commandments to save them from resting content with vague and often hypocritical sentiments, which – in ourselves and quite often even in other people – we are all of us prone to mistake for Christian love?[2]

What has just been said with reference to Romans 13.8–10 may also serve as a comment on the third passage (Gal. 5.14). But the fact that 'thou shalt love thy neighbour as thyself', contained in both Romans 13.9 and Galatians 5.14, is not a novel Christian insight but the law's own summary of its requirements with regard to human relations must not be forgotten. To deny that this is clear evidence that Paul saw the law as having a continuing validity for Christians strikes me as exceedingly perverse. Paul no doubt did believe that 'Christian love inevitably meets the standards set by the law' (p. 202) – if by 'Christian love' is meant *perfect* Christian love. But did he think that such perfect love was anywhere to be seen in the church on earth? I find it impossible to believe that the man who wrote Romans 1.18–3.20 had a 'retrospective' (p. 202) view, when he quoted Leviticus 19.18 (or, for that matter, the specific commandments also quoted in Rom. 13.9), and thought he was describing the actual conduct of Christians, not setting before them the goal towards which they have to strive lifelong.

Again, I am puzzled by p. 203, on which Westerholm seems to be suggesting that Paul thought (note the bold 'undoubtedly' at the top of the page!) that Christians are like the 'accomplished' or 'consummate' musician who has advanced beyond the stage of having to submit to the discipline of the elementary rules of music and now '"fulfills" the intention of the rules without always observing them' (p. 203). He claims that 'In a similar way, Paul can only believe that a life directed by God's Holy Spirit more than adequately "fulfills" the requirements of the law, even though specific demands have not been "done" and commands that are perceived to serve a purpose no longer have been ignored' (p. 203), and on p. 205 he actually states that 'For Paul it is important to say

---

[2] Cf. C. E. B. Cranfield, *A Critical and Exegetical Commentary on the Epistle to the Romans* 2, Edinburgh, [5]1989, p. 679.

that Christians "fulfill" the whole law, and thus to claim that their conduct (and theirs alone) fully satisfies the "real" purport of the law in its entirety . . .'. But is it conceivable that Paul, who was familiar with the law's own summary of its requirements, 'thou shalt love the LORD thy God with all thine heart, and with all thy soul, and with all thy might' (Deut. 6.5) and 'thou shalt love thy neighbour as thyself' (Lev. 19.18), could have thought that he himself or any of his fellow-Christians was in a position to claim that he 'more than adequately' fulfilled the law's requirements (p. 203), satisfied them 'completely' (p. 204), fulfilled 'the whole law' (p. 205), or that his conduct 'fully' satisfied 'the "real" purport of the law in its entirety' (p. 205)?

In this section Westerholm makes a lot of the distinction in usage which he sees between πληροῦν and ποιεῖν. This should, I think, be viewed with a considerable amount of caution. Would it not anyway have been more illuminating to have made the point that Paul can use πληροῦν with νόμον (or equivalent) both to denote the perfect obedience to the law which only Jesus has actually accomplished, and also to denote those beginnings of being turned in the direction of obedience which believers make in the freedom the Holy Spirit gives them?

II

In the third section of the chapter Westerholm attempts to establish the third position listed on p. 199 ('Paul consistently argues and assumes that Christians are no longer bound by the Mosaic code'). He claims at the start that 'the evidence that he [that is, Paul] believed Christians are free from the law is both explicit and abundant' (p. 205). It will be necessary first to look at the evidence he brings forward and then to look at some things which he does not mention, which seem to point to a different conclusion.

Westerholm appeals first to Romans 6.14f and 1 Corinthians 9.20; but, as it should not be assumed that ὑπὸ νόμον is used in the same way in both passages, we may look first at the Romans passage together with Romans 7.1–6 to which Westerholm refers on pp. 206–7. I have argued elsewhere[3] that in Romans 6.14b ('for ye are not under law, but under grace') Paul is thinking not of the law generally but of the law as condemning sinners, so of the law's condemnation. There seem to me to be a number of grounds for thinking this. First, the contrast between 'under law' (or probably better 'under the law') and 'under grace' can be said to support this explanation, since 'under God's condemnation' is a natural opposite to 'under grace' (i.e. God's grace or undeserved favour). Secondly, an assurance that Christians have been freed from God's condemnation seems a more apposite support (note the 'for' at the beginning of v. 14b) for the promise that sin shall no longer be lord over them than an assurance that they are altogether free from the law would be: confidence that one has been released from God's condemnation does indeed enable one to begin to resist sin's tyranny with courage and hopefulness. Thirdly, Romans 8.1 ('There is therefore now no condemnation to them that are in Christ Jesus') is surely strong support for this interpretation of οὐ ... ὑπὸ νόμον in 6.14, since it indicates that the point of 7.1–6, the significance of which it draws out (ἄρα νῦν), 7.7–25 being parenthetic, is the Christian's freedom from the law's condemnation, not from the law generally, and 7.1–6 seems to be naturally understood as connecting with 6.14b.

With regard to 1 Corinthians 9.20, it seems to me that the context suggests that Paul is here indicating not that he is not under the law at all, that it no longer has any validity for him, but that he is not under it in the same way as he had once been and as the non-Christian Jews are under it. Paul certainly recognized that there are very significant differences between the relation of Christians to the law and the relation of non-Christian Jews to it. Some of these will be noticed in the course of this essay. But one is particularly relevant here. Whereas for the non-Christian Jew the literal observance of the ceremonial law is still obligatory, the Christian, who knows that the One, to whom all along the law was pointing, has come and has accomplished his saving work, no longer has to observe it literally. (The word 'literally' in the last

[3] Op. cit. 1, ⁷1990, pp. 319–20.

sentence is important; for what is being suggested is not (*pace* Westerholm, e.g. pp. 200, 202, 203) that the ceremonial law has simply been abrogated and that the Christian should just ignore it, but that he should honour it by looking steadfastly in the direction in which it was all along pointing and by believing in Christ as he and his work are witnessed to by it.) But not all Christians understood this, and there were painful tensions in the church. Some insisted that all Christians must, for example, be circumcised, and their demands Paul strongly opposed. But there were others, who, while not trying to compel their fellow-Christians to follow their pattern, felt that, as far as they themselves were concerned, they could not with a clear conscience give up the observance of such requirements of the law as the distinction between clean and unclean foods, the avoidance of blood, the keeping of the Sabbath. Yet they were liable to give way to the social pressure of those of their fellow-Christians who were confident that they had this freedom, to the grievous detriment of their own integrity. Paul recognized their vulnerability, and was sensitive to it, as can be seen in Romans 14.1–15.13. Paul seems also to have tried to avoid giving unnecessary offence to non-Christian Jews, in connection with the ceremonial law. In view of what has just been said (perhaps also in view of the words μὴ ὤν ἄνομος θεοῦ ἀλλ᾽ ἔννομος Χριστοῦ in v. 21?), it would seem to be unwise to claim 1 Corinthians 9.20 as clear evidence that Paul thought that the law as a whole was no longer valid for him.

On p. 206 Westerholm claims that 'ye were made dead to the law through the body of Christ' in Romans 7.4 'clearly includes release from the law's demands'. But is this at all clear? Is it not more natural, in view of what Paul has said about Christians' dying with Christ in 6.1–11, and of what he had already said about the meaning of Christ's death in 3.21–26; 4.25; 5.6–11, 18–19, to take him to be referring to release from the law's condemnation through Christ's death for them?

With regard to Galatians 2.17–19, the exegetical problems involved are complicated, and there is far from being agreement about the thread of Paul's argument. If one sees a close connection between vv. 15–21 and vv. 11–14, in which Paul has related his public dispute with Peter in Antioch, one might well be inclined to think that the death to the law referred to in v. 19 has simply to do with observation of the ceremonial part of the law. The second and third clauses of vv. 19 and 20 might perhaps suggest that it is rather death to the law's condemnation. That Paul means death to the law generally is maintained by many; but it seems to me that this passage, taken by itself, provides a very insecure basis for holding that Paul saw the law as having no longer any validity for him.

Westerholm goes on to appeal to Galatians 3.19–4.5 as showing 'the temporal limitations on the law's validity' (p. 207). That Paul did indeed believe that there is a sense in which 'the epoch of the law has passed' may be readily agreed. We can speak of 'Old Testament times' or 'the Old Testament epoch' as of a period that is over and past, without implying that the Old Testament is no longer authoritative scripture for the Christian church. With the accomplishment of Jesus Christ's work the epoch of the law's unique authority had indeed come to an end; but it does not follow that the law had ceased to have validity for those who believe in him. Commandments like 'thou shalt have none other gods before me', 'thou shalt do no murder', 'thou shalt not bear false witness against thy neighbour', 'thou shalt love thy neighbour as thyself', did not cease to point the way to freedom and community and fulfilment, though they could now be more clearly recognized as God's fatherly guidance for his children. But Paul certainly thought that the relation of Christians to the law was very significantly different from that of non-Christian Jews to it.

Westerholm seems to say (p. 208) that, if Paul accepted that observance of the ritual law was no longer binding on Christians, he cannot have regarded any part of the law as binding on them, because, if he had, he would have felt the need to 'provide his churches with detailed instructions as to which commands they were obligated to observe and which they were not' and 'there is no evidence that he made any such distinctions. On the contrary, it is clear that, for Paul, Torah was a unit' (p. 208). But must not the distinction between ritual and moral have been clear to Paul? Is not Romans 7.7–25 illuminating in this connection? And Westerholm's argument from silence, from the absence of such detailed instructions as he refers to in the Pauline letters we possess, is surely precarious.

The further argument from 1 Corinthians 6.12ff and 10.23ff that 'Both the slogan itself [πάντα (μοι) ἔξεστιν] and Paul's non-legal way of qualifying it clearly indicate that the Christian is not thought to be obligated to observe the demands of the law' (p. 208) is scarcely cogent. Paul's quotation of the Corinthian libertines' slogan is not an unqualified endorsement of it, and the conclusion which Westerholm draws from the fact that Paul does not here appeal to any of the law's commands is by no means necessary. The specific commandments of the law are a guide for the gratitude of those who already know their indebtedness to God (cf. Exod. 20.2; Deut. 5.6); they are not themselves the ground of the believer's desire to obey them. The fact that Paul does not here adduce any commandments (in 1 Cor. 6.20 – 'ye were bought with a price' – he appeals to what is more basic than God's commands), does not at all prove that he did not think that the law still had validity for Christians.

Westerholm's final argument in this section is that Paul sees Christians as having to 'discover' the will of God 'for themselves as their mind is "renewed" and they grow in insight' (he appeals to Rom. 6.22; 12.2; Phil. 1.9–10), instead of relying on the guidance of the law, and that this 'shows clearly that the will of God is no longer defined as an obligation to observe the law's statutes' (p. 209). But, in answer to this, it may be said that use of the renewed mind and acceptance of the law's continuing validity are in no way incompatible, that Westerholm has already distorted the evidence by his treatment of the 'fulfilment' passages, Romans 8.4; 13.8–10; Galatians 5.14; and that such language as he has used in the last-quoted sentence is liable to give a very false impression of the position of those Christians who do think that the law has a continuing validity for them, suggesting, as it does, a wooden observance of the law's letter rather than a free and joyful aiming at its intention.

Some things which seem to me to be positive support for the view that Paul believed that the law still has a place in the life of Christians must now be mentioned. There is first the fact that he calls it God's law (Rom. 7.22, 25; 8.7: cf. (*pace* Westerholm, p. 201, n. 11) 1 Cor. 7.19): this is surely important. Must we not assume, unless there is quite conclusive evidence to the contrary, that Paul, if he recognized that the law was God's, is likely to have seen it as still valid for Christians? Secondly, there is the striking affirmation in Romans 7.12, 'So that the law is holy, and the commandment holy, and righteous, and good', to which Westerholm fails to pay the attention it deserves. I take it that Paul is affirming that both the law as a whole and its individual commandments are God's, that they are righteous both as directing human beings to try to act righteously and as manifesting God's own righteousness, and that they are intended to be beneficial to human beings. Is not this verse a very serious difficulty for those who maintain that Paul thought that the law no longer had any validity for Christians? Thirdly, his statement in Romans 7.14 that the law is 'spiritual' must be mentioned. It is surely an affirmation of its divine origin and by implication of its divine authority. Fourthly, Romans 7.14–25 as a whole must be mentioned; for, if those verses refer to the Christian life, as I am still convinced that they do,[4] they would seem to be strong support for the view that Paul saw a continuing role for the law in the church. For in this passage the law is depicted as guiding the obedience of the new ego which God is creating (note especially v. 25b). Fifthly, Romans 8.7 should be noted, since it seems to imply that those 'that are after the Spirit' should strive to be – and in some measure can be – 'subject to the law of God', in contrast with those whose life is characterized by 'the mind of the flesh'.

Sixthly, Paul's assertion in 1 Corinthians 7.19 that it is not circumcision or uncircumcision that matters 'but the keeping of the commandments of God' seems highly significant. Westerholm's contention (p. 201, n. 11) that by 'the commandments of God' Paul does not mean the commandments of the law, since 'the Mosaic law is not . . . in view in this chapter (the only "commandments" mentioned are Pauline and dominical;

---

[4] *Pace* N. T. Wright, *The Climax of the Covenant: Christ and the Law in Pauline Theology*, Edinburgh, 1991, pp. 196–225.

cf. vv. 10, 17, 25, and the frequent Pauline imperatives)', is unconvincing. Would Paul really be likely to refer to his own or indeed dominical commandments as ἐντολαὶ θεοῦ? And, if the commandments of the law are meant, the use of the word τήρησις is significant. Does it not indicate that Paul was not under the illusion that Christians no longer need to try to obey the law? But a comparison of the parallel statements in Galatians 5.6 and 6.15 is illuminating. For the πίστις δι' ἀγάπης ἐνεργουμένη of the former indicates something of what Paul understood to be involved in keeping the commandments of God, while the καινὴ κτίσις of the latter is a reminder that it is only as the Holy Spirit creates a new self in a human being that he or she is freed to begin to obey God's law.

Seventhly, there is the fact that the legislative elements of the Pentateuch were an integral part of what Paul knew and reverenced as Scripture. Westerholm, while accepting that Paul can use νόμος of the Pentateuch as a whole (e.g. in the phrase 'the law and the prophets' in Rom. 3.21) and also of the Old Testament as a whole (e.g. in Rom. 3.19; 1 Cor. 14.21), insists that νόμος 'in Paul's writings frequently (indeed, most frequently) refers to the sum of specific divine requirements given to Israel through Moses' (p. 108). But, while a verse like Galatians 3.17, which refers to the four hundred and thirty years between the making of the covenant and the giving of the law, makes it clear that Paul was aware of the different senses νόμος could have, have we really any justification for supposing that he thought of the law in this narrowest sense as something which could now be separated from its context in Scripture and assigned a value inferior to that of the rest of the Pentateuch? But, if he did regard it as an integral part of Scripture, we shall not arrive at a genuine solution to the problem of Paul's view of the law (in Westerholm's narrowest sense of the term) until we try to understand it within, rather than outwith, the framework of his view of the nature and authority of the Old Testament scriptures as a whole.

What has been said above seems to me to suggest strongly that Westerholm was much too quick to conclude that, for Paul, the law no longer has validity for Christians.

III

I turn now to the fourth section of Chapter X (headed 'The Letter and the Spirit').[5] The position it seeks to maintain was indicated on p. 199 thus: 'The mark of Christian ethics is life in the Spirit, an ethic which Paul explicitly contrasts with obligation to the law.' About the decisive importance of the Holy Spirit's part in the Christian life as Paul understood it there can, of course, be no doubt. It is the Holy Spirit who brings about the sanctification of believers. But it does not follow from this that Paul must have regarded 'walking in the Spirit' (so Westerholm, p. 214) or walking by the Spirit (cf. Gal. 5.16) as 'an ethical norm *replacing* the law' (p. 214). Paul knew the painful truth that Christians, though indeed indwelt by God's Spirit, do not always walk by the Spirit but often resist him and walk according to their own fallen human nature. He knew that they can be poor judges of the relative values of the various spiritual gifts, esteeming the showy and exciting ones above the more precious. He knew too that Christians are liable to be complacent, confident that they are already rich, already reigning (1 Cor. 4.8). In view of this I should need a lot of convincing that Paul could have thought of walking by the Spirit as an ethical norm replacing the law. Is not the Christian's experience of the Spirit something too individual, too liable to be mixed with the Christian's subjective thoughts, feelings, desires, to be a satisfactory ethical norm? The fact that Paul wanted the Corinthian Christians to learn 'not *to go* beyond the things which are written' (1 Cor. 4.6) and the fact that he has left us clear evidence of his own deep and constant engagement with the Old Testament scriptures lead me to think it much more likely that he regarded the law and, along with it, the rest of the Old Testament and also the tradition of the ministry and teaching of Jesus as the proper norm and standard of Christian conduct, a standard open and common to all believers, something objective, and that he thought of the Holy Spirit as the One who enables Christians rightly to

5 See also Westerholm's article, '"Letter" and "Spirit": the foundation of Pauline *Ethics*', in *NTS* 30 (1984), pp. 229–48.

understand the scriptures and the Jesus tradition and sets them free to begin to obey.

In his discussion of the letter–Spirit antithesis (pp. 209–13) he deals with Romans 2.27 (strangely, he ignores, apart from a footnote, 2.29, though it is in that verse and not in v. 27 that γράμμα and πνεῦμα actually occur together); Romans 7.6; and 2 Corinthians 3.6. Throughout this discussion he persists in attributing to those scholars, who believe that the Old Testament law still has a validity for Christians, an inclination to take γράμμα in these passages to mean a misunderstanding or a perversion of the law. There is an element of truth in this, and yet it is misleading and has the effect of setting up a straw man which can then be demolished without trouble. For a simple equation, γράμμα = 'a misunderstanding or a perversion of the law', clearly will not do. Had Westerholm read the passage[6] he quotes as representative of the view he is attacking and also its context more carefully, he might have recognized that its author was not suggesting quite so simplistic and unthought-through a solution as he supposes. Its author was, in fact, trying – however inadequately – to do justice both to the fact that οἴδαμεν ... ὅτι ὁ νόμος πνευματικός ἐστιν (Rom. 7.14) makes it extremely unlikely that Paul could intend a simple opposition between the Spirit and the law (so that a straight identification of γράμμα with the law is unsatisfactory) and also to the fact that γράμμα must indeed refer to the law itself. He therefore tried to suggest that, while γράμμα certainly refers to the law itself, it denotes the law itself as it is apart from that full and true effectiveness which it only possesses, when the Holy Spirit enables those who hear it truly to understand it in the light of Jesus Christ, and frees them to make a beginning of obeying it.

Westerholm, by contrast, understands Paul to use γράμμα to indicate the obligation on those under the law to obey it. So, with reference to Romans 7.6, he says: 'serving God by the "letter" must refer to the *obligation* of those subject to the old covenant to carry out the concrete commands of the law of God' (p. 212); and, with

---

[6] Cranfield, op. cit. 1, pp. 339–40.

reference to the three texts, Romans 2.27; 7.6; and 2 Corinthians 3.6, he says: 'Paul means seriously that those who lived under the law were obligated to fulfill the "letter"; indeed, the purpose of the law could only be achieved if those who were under its yoke were bound to observe its terms . . . Now, however, the way of the "letter" (i.e. obedience to the law) has become, for believers, a thing of the past; service is now rendered "in the new life of the Spirit" (Rom. 7.6)' (p. 213).

But in reply to Westerholm it must be said that the contrast Paul has in mind is not a contrast between a life lived under the obligation to try to obey the law and a life in which that obligation has been replaced by the guidance of the Spirit, but rather a contrast between the life of those, who, though possessing the law, have not yet been enabled by the Holy Spirit rightly to understand it in the light of Christ, and the life of those whom the Holy Spirit has both enabled to understand the law aright in the light of Jesus Christ and also set free to make a beginning of trying to obey it with humble joy.

With regard to the last section of Chapter X ('The Origin of Paul's View'), it seems to me that the sentence, 'Furthermore, since the law's demands cannot be detached from its sanctions, deliverance from the law's curse inevitably means freedom from its demands as well' (pp. 217f) is plainly fallacious. By what logic is it claimed that the law's demands cannot be detached from its sanctions? By what logic is it asserted that deliverance from the law's curse inevitably means freedom from its commands as well?

IV

In conclusion three brief observations may be made.

1. Westerholm seems inclined to assume that Paul must either have regarded the law as having no place in the Christian life or else have continued to find the will of God in it 'in the way he did as a Pharisee' (p. 214). But surely *tertium datur*! We may conclude that he continued to find the will of God in it, but did so now in a new and distinctively Christian way. It is of the utmost importance

that we do not underestimate the newness of the Christian's understanding of, and relation to, the law. He understands it in the light of Christ, in the light of his perfect obedience to it and of his clarification of its intention by his life and work and teaching. He has been freed from the illusion that he is able so well to fulfil it as to put God in his debt. He knows that, while it shows him the depth of his sinfulness, it no longer pronounces God's condemnation of him, since Christ has borne that condemnation for him. He no longer feels its commands simply as an obligation imposed on him from without, but is being set free by the Holy Spirit to desire wholeheartedly to try to obey and thereby to express his gratitude to God for his mercy and generosity. So he receives the law's commands as God's fatherly guidance for his children – not as a burden or an infringement of his liberty, but as the pointing out of the way to true freedom.

2. Westerholm seems to me to have failed to make any serious effort to understand the view of the law, which has been characteristic of, but by no means confined to, the Reformed churches and Reformed theology. It is noticeable that in his book Calvin gets not a single mention and Barth, I think, but half a line. The importance attached to the Decalogue in Christian education by such Reformed catechisms as the Geneva of 1541, the Heidelberg of 1563, the Westminster Larger and Shorter of 1648, is well known.[7] And in this matter of the place of the law in the life of Christians the Church of England has stood alongside the Reformed churches, as may be seen from the fact that in the 1662 Book of Common Prayer (as also in the 1552 Prayer Book) the rehearsing of the Ten Commandments has its place in the order of the Lord's Supper (note the repeated response, 'Lord, have mercy upon us, and incline our hearts to keep this law'), while both in Rite A and in Rite B of the Alternative Service Book of 1980 provision is made for either the Summary of the Law (itself, of

---

[7] An interesting recent example is J. M. Lochman, *Signposts to Freedom: the Ten Commandments and Christian ethics*, Belfast, Dublin, Ottawa, 1981 (English translation by David Lewis of *Wegweisung der Freiheit: Abriss der Ethik in der Perspektive des Dekalogs*, Gütersloh, 1979).

course, including two quotations from the law) or the Ten Commandments to be read. The view that Paul saw the law as having a continuing role in the life of Christians deserves a more sympathetic and careful consideration than Westerholm has given it.

3. It is perhaps wise to add – though it should surely go without saying – that to argue that the Old Testament law has a continuing validity in the Christian church does not at all mean that one ignores the great diversity of the materials which make it up (to treat them as a homogeneous code would, of course, be absurd) or denies the need for properly rigorous critical and historical study of it. It is possible to recognize that the law, like every other part of the Old Testament and also of the New, is from beginning to end the words of men and at the same time to take it seriously as God's law.[8]

---

[8] I tried to say something on the subject touched on in this paragraph in 'St Paul and the Law', in *SJT* 17 (1964), p. 67; but this was omitted for the sake of brevity in my ICC *Romans* 2 (cited above), p. 861.

10

Who Are Christ's Brothers (Matthew 25.40)?

The question of the identity of those referred to in Matthew 25.40, 45 as Christ's 'brothers' is not just a matter of academic interest. It is vitally important for the faith and life of the Christian church. Discussion of it has recently been re-opened by the publication in 1989 of Sherman W. Gray's *The Least of My Brothers: Matthew 25.31–46: A History of Interpretation*, Atlanta, Georgia, USA (Society of Biblical Literature Dissertation Series 114). Its first 351 pages are a remarkably comprehensive survey of the support over the centuries, from the end of the first century AD down to 1986, for the different answers given to this question and to the related question of the meaning of 'all the nations' in v. 32. This historical part of the book is very fully documented and has been written with admirable fairness and objectivity.

I

The results of Gray's historical study may be briefly summarized as follows.

In the patristic period, of the 504 references to the 'identity dialogue' (vv. 35–40, 42–45) investigated, 62% give no indication as to the identity of Christ's brothers, 33% restrict them to the Christian needy, and only 5% explicitly or implicitly include non-Christians among them. With regard to the meaning of 'all

* First published in *Metanoia* 4 (1994), pp. 31–39.

the nations', of the 114 Fathers investigated over 82% do not discuss the matter, fourteen witnesses support a universal interpretation, and six understand only Christians to be intended. In the Middle Ages (defined as 850–1399) the overwhelming majority of commentators restrict the brothers to Christians. Only four out of the twenty-one authors who comment on vv. 40 and 45 give any support to a non-restrictive view. The majority take 'all the nations' to mean all human beings, while a minority understand only Christians to be meant. In the period of the Renaissance and Reformation (1400–1699) out of the thirty-six authors commenting on vv. 40 and 45 twenty-nine take the brothers to be Christians and only five are definitely universalist. There is a near-consensus that 'all the nations' means everyone.

In the modern period the restrictive understanding of the brothers continues to dominate throughout the eighteenth century, sixteen out of twenty-three commentators identifying them as Christians and no commentator taking an explicitly universalist view. Fifteen interpreted 'all the nations' as meaning everyone; but for the first time the suggestion appears that the phrase means neither everyone nor Christians but all the heathen. The nineteenth century shows a considerable increase in support for the universalist view of the brothers, though the restrictive understanding is still predominant. At the same time, while the great majority of authors take 'all the nations' to mean all humankind, over 8% take it to mean all the heathen (i.e. all who are neither Christians nor Jews) and almost 10% all non-Christians (including Jews). In the twentieth century supporters of a non-restrictive view of the brothers (i.e. those understanding the needy generally together with those who do not indicate any restriction) for the first time outnumber those who support a restrictive sense, and, even when the neutrals are excluded, the explicit universalists still outnumber those who restrict the brothers to Christians (some premillennialists restrict not to Christians but to Jewish missionaries during 'the tribulation'). With regard to 'all the nations', nearly 65% of the authors investigated take it to mean all humankind, about 12% all who are neither Christians nor Jews, nearly 7% all non-Christians (so including Jews), a little over 8% only Christians, and 2% all non-Jews.

Whereas the first three periods furnished only 178 commentators on this pericope, in the modern period Gray found 736 authors (in over 800 works) with something to say on the subject. With regard to the identity of the brothers, of the 1409 references in all four periods together, 765 or close to 55% are neutral or non-restrictive. Throughout the centuries the narrow interpretation has the next strongest showing (almost 39%). The explicitly universal interpretation, though not seen in the second or the eighteenth century, is found in each of the four periods, and in the twentieth century becomes a close rival to the narrow view. With regard to 'all the nations', the majority opinion in all four periods is that it means all human beings. The only other view represented in all four periods is that Christians are meant. It is only in the modern period that the other views make their appearance: that the meaning is all non-Christians; that it is all who are neither Christians nor Jews; that it is all non-Jews.

Gray's historical study deserves to be warmly welcomed as an important and interesting contribution to New Testament scholarship. The accompanying bibliography is itself of great value (pp. 365–432). But his statement (pp. 351–64) of his own position on the exegesis of this passage (that the reference in vv. 40 and 45 is to Christians and that by 'all the nations' in v. 32 all non-Christians (including Jews) are meant) leaves us unconvinced. Since a strongly argued chapter ('Once More: Matthew 25.31–46') in Graham N. Stanton's impressive *A Gospel for a New People: Studies in Matthew*, Edinbugh, 1992, pp. 207–31, has come out firmly on Gray's side, we may consider the arguments, which these two authors advance, together.

II

We take first the arguments in support of the view that those to whom vv. 40 and 45 refer ('the least of these my brethren' and 'the least of these') are Christians.

(i) It is claimed that 'brother' (ἀδελφός) is firmly established in Matthew as a term for 'Christian disciple' (Gray, p. 357; Stanton, p. 216). That it can be so used is clear; but the evidence is far from proving that it is used in this way in Matthew 25.40. There are thirty-nine occurrences of ἀδελφός in Matthew. In twenty-one of these the word is used in its ordinary literal sense as in 4.18. Of the remaining eighteen occurrences there are eight in which it does denote a disciple: 12.48, 49, 50; 18.15 (twice), 21; 23.8; 28.10. In four of these (as in 25.40) a possessive is present ('my brother(s)'). But in 5.22 (twice), 23, 24; 7.3, 4, 5 ἀδελφός seems to mean 'neighbour', 'fellow Israelite'. In 18.35 'neighbour' or 'fellow man' seems to be the meaning (cf. 6.14–15, where 'men' (οἱ ἄνθρωποι) is used). In 5.47 the meaning of the word is uncertain: the evangelist could perhaps have in mind the members of the Christian community, but a reference to kinsfolk or to those who are fellow members of some other group would also seem to be possible (there is a variant reading which means 'friends'). The above evidence, while it certainly affords support for the view that the possibility that 25.40 may refer to Christians must be reckoned with, hardly goes further than this.

(ii) It is claimed that 'the least' (οἱ ἐλάχιστοι) is firmly established as a term for Christian disciples (Stanton, p. 216). Gray (p. 357) asserts that J. Winandy 'convincingly shows that whenever Jesus speaks of "little ones" or "the least", he refers to his disciples'. It is true that 'one of these little ones' occurs four times in Matthew (10.42; 18.6, 10, 14), and that each time Jesus is referring to his disciples (in one case the phrase is completed by 'that believe in me'). But, even if we admit that the four occurrences of 'these little ones' are enough to make 'little one' (μικρός) an established term for 'disciple' in Matthew, it is by no means clear that this also goes for the superlative ἐλάχιστος. It occurs five times in Matthew. It is used of Bethlehem in 2.5 ('by no means least among the rulers of Judah') and twice in 5.19 ('one of the least of these commandments'

and 'shall be called least in the kingdom of heaven'): the
two other occurrences are 25.40 and 45. The list of its
occurrences in Matthew would seem to be enough to
disprove the claim that οἱ ἐλάχιστοι is an established term
for the disciples in Matthew. It may be suggested that the
purpose of its use in 25.40 and 45 is not to insure that 'my
brothers' is understood to mean Christians but to insure
that it is understood in the widest possible sense – even the
most insignificant and most abject are included.

(iii) It is claimed that Jesus' identifying himself with his
disciples in Matthew 10.40 ('He who receives you receives
me') is support for taking 25.40 and 45 to refer to Christians
(Stanton, pp. 217–18). The same identification is made in
Acts 9.4–5; 22.7–8; 26.14–15. There is no need to doubt
that Jesus did identify himself with his disciples. But the
fact that he did so is not a good reason for denying that he
could also on occasion have identified himself with human
beings generally in their neediness.

(iv) For Stanton it is significant (pp. 210–11) that, if the narrow
interpretation of vv. 40 and 45 is taken (and 'all the nations'
understood as meaning all non-Christians), the passage
'reflects the social setting of Matthew's gospel which is
envisaged' in his book. He understands it as 'intended to
console anxious Christians who perceive themselves to be
threatened both by the local Jewish leadership and by
Gentile society at large'. But if the social setting of the
gospel was as Stanton believes – and we find much of his
book convincing – it still does not necessarily follow that
the evangelist must have thought that the best way to
console his fellow Christians was to assure them that in the
final judgment their non-Christian neighbours' treatment
of them would be the criterion by which those non-
Christians would be judged.

(v) Stanton relies heavily on the characterization of Matthew
25.31–46 as 'an apocalyptic discourse' (p. 221). He claims
that 'Since apocalyptic writings usually function as a consolation to groups of God's people who perceive themselves

to be under threat or alienated from the society in which they live, this is likely to be the central thrust of Matt. 25.31–46' (p. 222), and goes on to assert: 'The relationship between Matthew 25 and apocalyptic writings which were also written towards the end of the first century strengthens considerably the interpretation of Matthew's final judgment scene which I am defending' (p. 223). He then (pp. 224–8) quotes extensively from 4 Ezra (4.23; 7.37–38: he also cites 5.23–30; 6.57–59; 12.31–33; 13.37); 2 Baruch (72.2–73.1); and 1 Enoch (62.3, 9–12; 103.9–15; 104.1–4), after first quoting Joel 3.1–3, which he regards as the *locus classicus* for the apocalyptic motif he is concerned with, namely, the coming judgment of the nations on the basis of their treatment of God's people. That this motif is illustrated in these writings is, of course, true. But what Stanton fails to recognize is that what distinguishes the Matthew passage from these writings may be more significant than what connects it with them. For one thing, is there not a striking contrast between the austere simplicity, the 'sobriety of feature and colour', the 'reserve' and even 'bareness',[1] of this passage and what is characteristic of Jewish and indeed Christian apocalypses? And is it not significant that in Matthew 25.31ff it is to the blessedness to come to those who had shown compassion to Christ's brothers rather than to the punishment to fall on those who had failed to show compassion that prominence is given? And also that the distresses referred to are ones anybody might suffer, not ones which Christians are particularly likely to suffer because they are Christians, such as persecution? When the special features of this passage are taken into account, it becomes apparent how perilous it is to draw conclusions from the apocalyptic writings about what 'is likely to be the central thrust of Matt. 25.31–46'.

[1] The language is derived from T. Preiss, *Life in Christ*, London, 1954 (translated from *La Vie en Christ*, Neuchâtel, 1952), p. 47.

The main argument in favour of taking 'all the nations' in v. 32 to mean the non-Christian world, all non-Christians, is that τὰ ἔθνη ('the nations') is never used in Matthew to refer to Christians or to Christians and non-Christians together, but always refers to Gentiles over against Christians or Jews (Stanton, p. 214). But this contention cannot be allowed to pass unchallenged. There are ten occurrences of τὰ ἔθνη in Matthew. In the four of these, in which it is preceded by πάντα ('all'), that is in 24.9, 14; 28.19, and the verse we are concerned with, we can see no good reason for denying that the meaning is 'all mankind'. In the case of 24.9 ('you will be hated by all nations for my name's sake') it is interesting to compare the wording of 10.22 ('you will be hated by all for my name's sake'), and in 24.14 the fact that 'to all nations' is used in association with 'throughout the whole world' would seem to tell in favour of its meaning 'all humankind' rather than 'all non-Christians'. And in 28.19 too 'all nations' surely means 'all human beings': the evangelist is hardly likely to have been so pedantic as to mean to exclude Christians on the ground that those who are already disciples do not need to be made disciples. We conclude that this argument of Stanton and others should be rejected.

III

What then can be said in support of understanding Christ's 'brothers' in vv. 40 and 45 as the needy generally and all the nations' in v. 32 as meaning all humankind?

(i) The relation of this pericope to its immediate context in the Eschatological Discourse (chapters 24 and 25) points to this interpretation. In the latter part of this discourse the evangelist's skilful and purposive workmanship is clear to see. In place of the last five verses of Mark 13 we have in Matthew fifty-six verses (24.42–25.46). What we get is a powerful exposition of what Jesus' command to watch (Mark 13.33, 35, 37) means for the church in the time before the Parousia. Mathew 24.3 has already underlined the fact that it is to the disciples, that is, to the church that this discourse is addressed. After the call to watch (24.42) we get the parable of the householder (vv. 43–44); the parable of the servant who may prove either faithful or evil (vv. 45–51); the parable of the ten virgins (25.1–14); the parable of the talents (vv. 14–30); and finally the passage with which we are concerned. The decision between faithfulness and unfaithfulness is the subject of 24.45–51; and the three pericopae of chapter 25 are closely bound together by the fact that in each of them there is a decisive separation of human beings. What we have in all of 24.42–25.46 is exhortation addressed to disciples, to Christians, so truly and faithfully to watch for Christ that they may be ready for him when he comes. To argue that there is a significant 'break in the thrust of the discourse' between vv. 30 and 31, on the ground that 'it is no longer solely Christians who are being addressed, but men and women in general', as Stanton does (p. 222), is unconvincing; for the fact that 'all the nations' are mentioned in v. 32 does not imply that others besides Christians are actually being directly addressed. To interpret this pericope as intended to console Christians by assuring them that non-Christians will be judged on the basis of whether or not they have shown them kindness is surely to destroy the closely-knit unity of 24.42–25.46. But to see it as further exhortation, as a further exposition of what it means to watch – that the watching required must include recognizing and serving Christ as he comes in the meantime in the persons of all needy and suffering human beings – is to do justice to it as the fitting climax of the Eschatological Discourse. And, if these verses are exhortation to Christians to watch properly, then that must mean that those addressed are to see themselves among those who are going to be judged: so 'all the nations' in v. 32 must include Christians and cannot denote just the non-Christian world.

(ii) The relation of this pericope to the structure of Matthew as a whole also points to this interpretation. As the last paragraph of the Eschatological Discourse, it is also the

climax of all the five discourses or collections of Jesus'
teaching in Matthew. How important these are for the
evangelist is clear from the way each of them is marked off
by a careful concluding formula (7.28; 11.1; 13.53; 19.1;
26.1). As each of them is preceded by narrative material or
by a combination of narrative and debate material, the
whole of 3.1–25.46 is Matthew's account of the deeds and
words of Jesus. So this pericope stands as the climax of that
whole account and immediately precedes the Passion
narrative. Is it likely that the evangelist, who has already
included such teaching as 5.43–48; 6.14f; 18.21–35 and
whose arrangement of his material is careful and purposive,
would place at this point a passage designed to console
Christians by assuring them that non-Christians are
going to be judged at the last according to whether or
not they have been kind to Christians? Would it not be
– for anyone who has followed attentively what has
gone before – an incredible anticlimax? To offer such a
consolation would surely be to reinforce those powerful
tendencies to self-centredness and self-complacency,
against which Christians and the church as a whole have
always to struggle. By contrast, on the interpretation for
which we are arguing, 25.31–46, as a call to Christians to
recognize Christ as he comes to them in the persons of their
suffering fellow human beings, is a fitting culmination of
what has gone before and a not inappropriate prelude to
the narrative of the Passion of him who 'came not to be
served but to serve, and to give his life as a ransom for
many'.

(iii) The use of the superlative ἐλάχιστος ('least') in vv. 40 and
45 perhaps tells in favour of taking those referred to as
brothers to be the needy and suffering generally. For, while
its use with regard to this vast multitude of the easily
ignored and forgotten, in order to make the point that not
even one of them, however insignificant, is forgotten by
Christ, is understandable, its use with regard to Christians
would be less easy to understand, since it would be taken

for granted in the church that all Christians are of value to Christ.

(iv) If the evangelist thought that those referred to in vv. 40 and 45 must be Christians, it is perhaps surprising that he has given no hint at all of this. He does not seem to have felt inhibited from giving editorial interpretative hints elsewhere (a good example of such a hint is in 21.39, where he has altered the order of Mark 12.8 ('they took him and killed him, and cast him out of the vineyard') to 'they took him and cast him out of the vineyard, and killed him'). There is absolutely nothing here to indicate that it was because they were Christians that these brothers were hungry, thirsty, strangers, naked, sick or in prison.

(v) It is clear that, while all the individuals included in 'all the nations', whether we take that phrase to mean all human beings (which is what we think) or all Gentiles or all non-Christians, could be assumed to have had some opportunity to succour a fellow human being in distress, they could not all be assumed to have had a chance to succour a Christian in distress. So, if the brothers are limited to Christians, such a succouring or not succouring could not be a universally applicable criterion. This seems a strong ground for understanding the brothers to be the needy generally.

(vi) The fact that other New Testament references to eschatological judgment (e.g. Acts 10.42; 17.31; Rom. 2.16; 3.6; 14.10–12; 2 Cor. 5.10; 1 Pet. 4.5; Rev. 20.11–13) seem to lend no support to the idea of a judgment which excludes Christians is an argument for rejecting the view that 'all the nations' in v. 32 means non-Christians.

We conclude that, at any rate as far as the evangelist's intention is concerned,[2] it is the needy and suffering of this world generally

---

[2] In this essay I have concentrated on the evangelist's understanding of this passage. I have done so, because I recognize that exegesis has to start with the evangelist's intention, not because I am not interested in whether we have Jesus'

who are referred to in this passage as Christ's brothers and 'all the nations' means all humankind including Christians. The passage is exhortation addressed to Christians. It continues the exposition of the meaning of the watching commanded in 24.42. It discloses the mystery of the presence of Christ in the time before the Parousia in the persons of the least of his brothers and sisters. In this judgment scene the righteous and the unrighteous alike are depicted as not having known who it was with whom they had had to do. But the purpose of the passage is that those who are being addressed may not remain ignorant of the mystery, but may recognize their King as he comes to them now in the persons of their suffering fellow human beings and render him loving service.

---

own teaching here. I do, as a matter of fact, think that we are very close to Jesus himself in this passage; but to try to show that this is so is outside the purpose of this essay. For a more expository treatment of this passage I might refer to a Cambridge University sermon published in *London Quarterly and Holborn Review* 186 (1961), pp. 275–81, reprinted in my *If God be for us: a collection of sermons*, Edinburgh, 1985, pp. 97–111.

11

The Resurrection
of Jesus Christ

About the importance accorded to the resurrection of Jesus Christ
in the New Testament there can hardly be any doubt. It is referred
to explicitly and with emphasis in seventeen of the twenty-seven
books. These seventeen include all four Gospels, the Acts of the
Apostles, Romans and 1 and 2 Corinthians,[1] while the ten which
do not explicitly mention it include the seven shortest and slightest
books.[2] And those New Testament books, which contain no explicit
reference to the Resurrection, may anyway be said to imply it. It
may truly be said that they 'breathe the Resurrection'.[3] Without
the existence of belief in Jesus as risen from the dead, their
existence is hardly explicable.

Many passages indicate very clearly the centrality of the
Resurrection. One of the most striking is Romans 10.9 ('Because
if thou shalt confess with thy mouth Jesus *as* Lord, and shalt
believe in thy heart that God raised him from the dead, thou
shalt be saved'); for it makes it abundantly clear that, for Paul,
belief that God has raised Jesus from the dead is the decisive and

---

* First published in *The Expository Times* 101 (1989–90), pp. 167–72.

[1] The rest of the seventeen are Galatians, Ephesians, Philippians, Colossians,
1 Thessalonians, 2 Timothy, Hebrews, 1 Peter and Revelation. (On the fact that
the only direct reference to the Resurrection of Christ in Hebrews is in 13.20 see
C. E. B. Cranfield, *The Bible and Christian Life*, Edinburgh, 1985, p. 146.)

[2] Namely, 2 Thessalonians, Titus, Philemon, 2 Peter, 2 and 3 John and Jude.

[3] The Epistle of James might seem to be an exception; but on it see Cranfield,
op. cit., pp. 151ff.

characteristic belief of Christians. Similarly clear is his statement in 1 Corinthians 15.14 that 'if Christ hath not been raised, then is our preaching vain, your faith also is vain'. We may set beside these Pauline examples the words of 1 Peter 1.3 ('Blessed *be* the God and Father of our Lord Jesus Christ, who according to his great mercy begat us again unto a living hope by the resurrection of Jesus Christ from the dead') and the characterization by the author of Acts of the apostles' preaching as 'their witness of the resurrection of the Lord Jesus'.[4] If then the Resurrection is so central to the faith of the New Testament, it clearly matters tremendously whether the affirmation that Jesus was raised from the dead is true or not. If our study of the New Testament is serious, we are bound sooner or later to ask, 'Was Jesus of Nazareth really raised from the dead?' Can we, or can we not, respond to the Easter greeting, 'Christ is risen', with our own 'He is risen indeed', with intellectual and moral integrity?

I shall attempt here, first, to consider the main objections urged against the truth of the affirmation that Jesus was raised from the dead; secondly, to set out the main arguments which may be brought in support of it; and, thirdly, to indicate the conclusion to which I personally come.

I

1. The New Testament contains no narrative of the actual raising of Jesus (according to the New Testament that was an event which no mortal eye saw), but it does contain several accounts of incidents associated with it, namely, the discovery of the empty tomb and the resurrection appearances. The first of the objections which have to be considered is that there are a number of apparent discrepancies between these accounts.

   (i) Luke 23.56 seems to indicate that it was before the sabbath began that the women prepared their spices and ointments, whereas according to Mark 16.1 they waited till the sabbath was over before buying their spices.

[4] Acts 4.33; cf. 1.22; 2.32; 3.15; 5.32; 10.41; 13.31.

(ii) As to the time when the women came to the tomb on the first day of the week, Mark surprisingly qualifies his 'very early' by 'when the sun was risen', which seems to contradict it (the Western variant which gives the sense 'as the sun was rising' looks like an attempt to remove the difficulty). The 'at early dawn' of Luke 24.1 and 'while it was yet dark' of John 20.1 agree with Mark's 'very early', but not with his 'when the sun was risen'. Matthew's 'late on the sabbath day, as it began to dawn toward the first day of the week' (28.1) would seem to indicate Saturday evening after sundown, when (according to Jewish reckoning) the first day of the week was beginning.

(iii) According to Mark 16.1 (compare Luke 24.1) the women's purpose was to anoint the body; but Matthew 28.1 gives as their intention simply 'to see the sepulchre'.

(iv) As to the number and names of the women who came to the tomb there is a puzzling variation. According to Mark there were three, Mary Magdalene, Mary the mother of James, and Salome; according to Matthew 28.1 there were two, Mary Magdalene and 'the other Mary'. Luke 24.10 names three women, two of whom are the same as in Mark, while Joanna replaces Salome (there is also a reference to 'the other women with them'). According to John 20.1, 11 and 18, Mary Magdalene was apparently alone.[5]

(v) According to Mark 16.5 and Matthew 28.5, one angel appears to the women: in Luke 24.4 (compare v. 23) and John 20.12 two angels are seen.

(vi) The effect of the angel's (or angels') words on the women is variously represented. Mark 16.8 tells us that the women 'went out, and fled from the tomb; for trembling and astonishment had come upon them: and they said nothing to any one; for they were afraid'. Matthew also mentions their fear, but couples with it 'great joy', and adds that they 'ran to bring his disciples word' (28.8). Luke says that they

---

[5] Though the first person plural in John 20.2 ('we know not') is possibly a trace of the involvement of more than one woman.

returned from the tomb, and told all these things to the eleven, and to all the rest' (24.9). In John the angels do not give the command, but Jesus himself gives it and Mary obeys.

(vii) In contrast with all four Gospels, Paul says nothing of any visit of women (or of a woman) to the tomb.

(viii) While all four Gospels testify to the tomb's being empty, Paul does not mention the tomb at all.

(ix) 1 Corinthians 15.5 seems to imply that the first person to see the risen Lord was Peter. Luke 24.34 agrees with this. But Matthew 28.9 (compare 28.1), John 20.14–17 and the Markan appendix (Mark 16.9) agree that Jesus appeared first either to Mary Magdalene alone or to her and 'the other Mary'. Mark 16.1–8 says nothing about an appearance of Jesus himself to the women.

(x) Mark 14.28 and 16.7 point to a resurrection appearance in Galilee, though Mark's own text stops at 16.8 without any appearance's having been related. Matthew does record such an appearance (28.16ff), preceded by one to the women in Jerusalem (28.9f). John 20 relates appearances in Jerusalem, John 21 appearances in Galilee. Luke stands apart somewhat awkwardly, in that he not only records appearances only in Jerusalem and its neighbourhood, but also by his omission of any parallel to Mark 14.28, his pointed alteration of Mark 16.7 (Luke 24.6f) and his inclusion of the command to tarry in Jerusalem in 24.49 (compare Acts 1.4) seems to be deliberately ruling out the possibility of a Galilean appearance.

Some further discrepancies can be discerned; but these which have been listed would seem to be the most significant. Of these the first six are not, I think, particularly serious. Differences between the accounts of eye-witnesses of quite ordinary events are a common enough phenomenon. And, if the Resurrection really did happen, the incidents associated with it were certainly not just ordinary events. That there should be signs of disturbance and strain in the human testimony would not be surprising. With regard to (vii), we need not infer that Paul did not know of the part played by the women. His omission of them in 1 Corinthians 15.4ff is adequately explained on the assumption that he specially wanted to cite witnesses who would be as generally acceptable as possible. In Jewish legal practice women were not accepted as credible witnesses except in certain limited areas of life, and in Gentile society too their position in regard to the law was inferior to that of men.[6] With regard to (viii), Paul's omission of any reference to the tomb goes naturally with his not mentioning the women as witnesses. To conclude from it that Paul and the earliest tradition must have known nothing of the empty tomb is quite unjustifiable. The emptiness of the tomb is almost certainly implied by the mention of burial between 'died' and 'hath been raised' in 1 Corinthians 15.4. With regard to (ix), the disagreement as to who was the first to see the risen Lord, the part played by concern that the testimony should be generally acceptable is to be recognized. With regard to (x), it is to be noted that Luke, who appears to be intent on excluding the tradition of appearances in Galilee, is also the one who, by specifying forty days as the period between the resurrection and the ascension, underlines the fact that there was ample time to allow for appearances both in Jerusalem and its neighbourhood and also in Galilee.

2. The presence of an angel or angels in the Gospel Easter narratives is probably for a good many people an additional reason for doubting the truth of the Resurrection. On this it may simply be said that, while angels as generally depicted in Christian art are indeed incredible, the possibility that the angels of the Bible may be a quite different matter should not be ignored. It would be wise at least to consider Karl Barth's discussion of the angels in *Church Dogmatics* III/3, pp. 369–519,[7] before we decide either to dismiss the Easter angel as a legendary accretion or to appeal to his presence in the story as a reason for rejecting the truth of the Resurrection itself.

[6] That Paul's not mentioning the women here was due to a personal antipathy to women is disproved by, among other things, the notable prominence of female names in Romans 16.

[7] For a brief account of this, reference may be made to W. A. Whitehouse, *The Authority of Grace*, Edinburgh, 1981, pp. 47–52.

3. But the most important objection of all is, without doubt, simply the apparent sheer, stark, utter impossibility of the thing. For Jews of New Testament times, who believed in the final, eschatological resurrection, the idea that that final resurrection had, in the case of one man, been accomplished already was unthinkable. For the vast multitudes of modern men and women, to whom it seems perfectly obvious that death is the end, the manifest, incontrovertible, irreversible termination of a human life, the claim that Jesus was raised from the dead is nonsense, its folly apparent as soon as it is uttered. And this conviction that death is the end does seem to give modern man a certain sense of security. At least, when things are going well for him, he can enjoy his brittle triumphs, strut a while in pride and forget about his limits. But the message of the Resurrection threatens even this illusory sense of security. It opens up a vast vista of the unknown, mocking man's self-importance. To entertain the thought of it is to suffer all one's ordinary preconceptions to be called in question. No wonder it is so earnestly resisted. Whether this third and strongest objection is outweighed by what will be set out below remains to be seen.

II

The main things which may be said in support of the truth of the Resurrection must now be indicated.

1. The transformation of the disciples may be mentioned first. There is no reason to question the historicity of their frightened and dejected condition at the time of the death of Jesus, as portrayed in the Gospels (e.g. Mark 14.50, 66–72; John 20.19). It is not something which the early church would have been inclined to invent. Besides, it is something we could safely have taken for granted, even without the testimony of the Gospels, as the natural, the inevitable, consequence of what they had experienced. But it is evident that within a few weeks of the Crucifixion these same disciples had become bold and energetic witnesses of a risen Christ. Leaving aside the testimony of the early chapters of Acts, we have firm enough evidence of this transformation in what Paul says of his own persecution of the church (1 Cor. 15.9; Gal. 1.13). Already

within – at the very most – five or six years of the Crucifixion so many had been won by the disciples' witness, that the young Pharisee was moved to mount a strenuous and energetic campaign against the followers of Jesus. This astounding transformation of the disciples presupposes a sufficient cause, something which was enough to convince them that Jesus was alive.

2. The second piece of evidence is the conversion and subsequent life and work of the apostle Paul. His most extended testimony to the fact of the Resurrection is in 1 Corinthians 15. Here, writing in AD 53 or 54 (more than a decade before the earliest of the Gospels), he reminds the Corinthian Christians of the tradition which he had passed on to them when he was in Corinth (probably in AD 50–51). As he indicates that the tradition he passed on he had himself received, the implication would seem to be that what is said in the latter part of v. 3 and in vv. 4–7 is the church's basic tradition which he had received in the earliest days of his Christian life. In v. 8 he adds his personal testimony: 'And last of all, as unto one born out of due time,[8] he appeared also to me.' In connection with Paul's conversion a number of points must be made.

---

[8] The sense of 'as unto one born out of due time' is uncertain. Is Paul alluding to the difference between his seeing the risen Lord after the Ascension and the pre-Ascension Resurrection appearances? But the natural significance of *ektroma* has to do not with unduly late, but with unduly early, birth, denoting that which is not yet properly formed and ready to be born. C. K. Barrett, *A Commentary on the First Epistle to the Corinthians*, London, 1968, p. 344, suggests that it could be said that 'in comparison with other apostles who had accompanied Jesus during his ministry he had been born without the due period of gestation'. Could it perhaps be that Paul's thought is rather of the fact that he was still a furious persecutor of the disciples when he was apprehended by Christ – so in a real sense extremely unprepared, something not properly formed, an ugly thing? The way Paul continues in v. 9 (note the 'For') might seem to support this suggestion: 'For I am the least of the apostles, that am not worthy to be called an apostle. because I persecuted the church of God.' This seems preferable both to the suggestion that Paul is taking up a reproach levelled against him by his opponents and also to the suggestion that Paul means 'that he has seen by anticipation the glory of Christ as that will be manifest in the *Parousia*' (S. Neill and T. Wright, *The Interpretation of the New Testament 1861-1986*, Oxford, 1988, p. 308, n. 1).

(i)   It cannot be maintained at all plausibly that this zealous persecutor of the disciples was in any way predisposed to accept the truth of the Resurrection. Having committed himself so publicly to the attempt to root out the new movement as something mischievous, he had a personal interest in not believing. For him to accept that Jesus had been raised from the dead was a volte-face involving a high degree of personal humiliation.

(ii) As one who had been working in conjunction with the Jewish authorities, he is likely to have been well acquainted with their views on the ministry of Jesus and subsequent events. He must surely have known what answer or answers they were giving to the claim that he was risen.

(iii) His unquestionable intellectual power (about which no one who has been at all seriously engaged in the study of the Epistle to the Romans is likely to have any doubts) must be taken into account.

(iv) He was clearly a deeply religious man, fully aware how serious a thing it would be to bear false witness about God by proclaiming that God raised Jesus from the dead, if in fact he did not raise him (compare 1 Cor. 15.15). The testimony of this man, with his background, his qualities, his character, with his mind which has left us so much authentic evidence of its workings (in – at the very least – 1 and 2 Corinthians, Galatians and Romans), I personally find extraordinarily convincing.

3. A third thing to mention is the striking prominence of women in the Gospel Easter narratives. Reference has already been made, in connection with Paul's omitting female witnesses in 1 Corinthians 15.4ff, to the fact that women were not acceptable witnesses in Jewish legal practice. It made sense to cite only those whose testimony stood a real chance of being taken seriously. The fact that these traditions, in which women featured so prominently, were nevertheless preserved would seem to indicate the presence of a high regard for historical truthfulness. That such traditions could be inventions of the community seems inconceivable, since

they flouted accepted ideas about credible witness, were liable to attract ridicule[9] and, furthermore, ran counter to the natural tendency to magnify the apostles (since they represent the women as receiving the news of the Resurrection before them). This third thing, then, which is inexplicable except as genuine historical reminiscence, would seem to be a further pointer to the truth of the Resurrection.

4. The undisputed fact that, in spite of all that the sabbath meant to Jews and although Jesus himself had loyally observed it all his life (even if not always in such a way as to satisfy his critics), Jewish as well as Gentile Christians soon came to regard the first day of the week as the special day for Christian worship[10] is highly significant. The replacement of sabbath by Lord's day presupposes a sufficient cause – nothing less than, at the very least, an extraordinarily strong conviction of an event's having taken place on the first day of the week which could be seen as transcending in importance even God's 'rest' after completing his work of creation.

5. Another thing to be said in support of the truth of the Resurrection is that, before the event, neither the women nor the disciples had the slightest expectation of their Master's being raised from the dead before the general eschatological resurrection. The early church, convinced that Jesus had been raised, certainly searched the Old Testament for passages which could be taken to foretell the Resurrection: but there is no reason to believe that the Old Testament had suggested to the disciples, before the first Easter Day, any hope of this sort. That the various predictions of the Passion (in particular, Mark 8.31; 9.31; 10.32–34), if in their present form made by Jesus himself (something which is, of course,

---

[9] We catch a glimpse in the New Testament itself of the sort of ridicule which could have been expected, in the reference to 'old wives' fables' in 1 Timothy 4.7 and in what is said about the fecklessness of 'silly women' and the ease with which they can be led astray in 2 Timothy 3.6f. For material illustrative of ancient Jewish, Greek and Roman attitudes to women reference may be made to the article on γυνή in G. Kittel and G. Friedrich (ed.), *TWNT*, Stuttgart, 1933–79, Vol. 1 (Eng. tr. by G. W. Bromiley, *TDNT*, 1964ff).

[10] Cf. Acts 20.7; 1 Corinthians 16.2; Revelation 1.10 (perhaps); Didache 14.1.

strongly denied by many), were not understood by the disciples at the time, seems clear enough.

6. There is also the highly significant fact that neither the Jewish nor the Roman authorities ever produced evidence to disprove the claim that Jesus had been raised. The Jewish authorities, in particular, had every reason to want to do so, and they must surely have been in a position to interrogate and search thoroughly. Rumours of what the disciples were saying can scarcely have failed to get to the ears of authority within a few days of the Crucifixion, even if the audacious public proclamation of the Resurrection did not start till Pentecost. The chances of finding the body, if the claim that Jesus was risen was not true, must surely at that early date have been quite good. The Sanhedrin must have known that the most effective way to be rid of what they regarded as a dangerous movement would be to produce the body, and knowing this they must surely have instituted an energetic search. The fact that with the will and the powers and resources they surely had, they never produced the body must count as a significant consideration in favour of the truth of the Resurrection.

7. Last of all must be mentioned the continuance of the Christian church through nineteen and a half centuries, in spite of bitter and often prolonged persecution, in spite of all its own terrible unworthiness and incredible follies, in spite of its divisions, and in spite of all the changes which the passing years and centuries have brought. The fact that the church still produces today (as it has produced in all the past centuries of its existence) human beings, who, trusting in Jesus Christ crucified, risen and exalted, show in their lives, for all their frailty, a recognizable beginning of being freed from self for God and neighbour, is a not unimpressive pointer to the truth of the Resurrection.

III

It will, I think, be helpful at this point to attempt some clarification of the two basic alternatives between which we have to choose: (*a*) Jesus was raised from the dead; and (*b*) Jesus was not raised from the dead. With regard to (*a*), it must be said that we are concerned with the affirmation *of the New Testament and of the church's creeds* that Jesus *was raised*. We must therefore put aside two views of the Resurrection which are sometimes proposed: first, that according to which it is possible to believe in the Resurrection without believing that the crucified body was raised; and, secondly, that which insists that the risen body is simply the crucified body resuscitated, possessed of exactly the same properties as it had before death. Both these views must, I believe, be rejected as inconsistent with the witness of the New Testament. In support of the former, appeal is made to Paul's failure to mention the empty tomb; but the sequence 'died . . . was buried . . . hath been raised' in 1 Corinthians 15.3f surely implies it, as does Paul's use of the language of 'raising' here and elsewhere. It would seem that there never was in the early church a belief in the Resurrection which did not involve belief that the tomb was empty. A supposed belief in the Resurrection without belief that the tomb was empty must surely be classified as acceptance of basic alternative (*b*), not as acceptance of basic alternative (*a*). As to the latter view, it is contradicted by the way the New Testament represents the risen Jesus as appearing and vanishing, becoming less or more recognizable (e.g. Luke 24.16, 31; John 20.14–16), and passing through closed doors (John 20.19, 26: cf. vv. 6 and 7, in which it seems to be suggested that the body had been mysteriously withdrawn from the cloths, leaving them collapsed where they were). The New Testament attests the risen body's being the same body as was crucified (Luke 24.39–40; John 20.27), but the same body wonderfully changed, transformed into a glorious body, no longer subject to the limitations of Jesus' historical life.[11]

With regard to basic alternative (*b*), clarification is achieved when we recognize that to accept it means coming to one of three

[11] It is scarcely fair to press Luke 24.42f and Acts 10.41 as proof that the author of Luke and Acts must have entertained a different view. Why should we assume that he could not have thought that the risen Jesus could partake of earthly food and drink, not because his risen body needed them, but for the sake of his disciples?

conclusions: either, the church's belief that Jesus was raised from the dead is based on a fraud; or, it is based on a mistake; or, it is based on some combination of fraud and mistake. It would seem, then, that there are, in all, four alternatives from which we have to choose:

(i) The Christian affirmation of the Resurrection has its origin in a fraud;

(ii) It has its origin in a mistake;

(iii) It has its origin in some sort of combination of fraud and mistake;

(iv) It is true.

With regard to (i), Matthew 27.62–66 and 28.11–15 are evidence that the explanation of the Resurrection as a fraud perpetrated by the disciples, who had stolen the body of Jesus and then announced that he had been raised from the dead, was current among the Jews at the time of the composition of Matthew. We may accept that, were a fraud really at the bottom of the matter, the disciples (and the women) would be the only – even remotely – likely perpetrators of it. No one else is at all likely to have had an interest in the propagation of such a falsehood. The Jewish and Roman authorities had, in fact, a very strong interest in Jesus's being securely dead. But the objections to this first alternative are formidable indeed. What motive could the disciples have had for embarking upon such a fraud? Is it really likely that they would have succeeded not only in disposing of the body (in the circumstances, perhaps itself not a very easy task) but also in convincing a large number of people that they had seen the risen Jesus (1 Cor. 15.5–8)? Do not the discrepancies and unevennesses between the various accounts of the visits to the tomb and of the Resurrection appearances weigh against the credibility of such a theory (one would have expected the perpetrators of a concerted deception to have taken more care to make their stories agree)? Would such a fraud account for that transformation of the disciples to which reference has already been made? And, last and most telling of all, is it possible to reconcile responsibility for the conception and carrying out of such a fraud with what we know of the character and conduct of the earliest Christians?[12]

Alternative (ii) can take more than one form. There is the explanation of the Resurrection appearances as hallucinatory experiences. But there is no evidence to suggest that the disciples or the women were in such a state of mind as would have made them liable to this sort of hallucination. They were not expecting any resurrection before the final one at the end of history (the reflection attributed to the chief priests and Pharisees in Matthew 27.63 hardly accords with the disciples' understanding of Jesus' teaching during his ministry); and their Jewish background would hardly have made them susceptible to such hallucinations. Moreover, the experiencing of hallucinations by so many different individuals and groups as are listed in 1 Corinthians 15.5–8 or are represented in the Gospels as seeing the risen Jesus, and in such varied situations, is hard to envisage. There is also the suggestion that the women went to the wrong tomb by mistake. But it is extremely difficult to imagine how the mistake would not have been quickly corrected. Is it really plausible to maintain that the transformation of the disciples was simply the result of a misunderstanding or of an illusion born of hallucination? Does such an explanation of belief in the Resurrection do justice to the fact that the earliest church included at any rate one or two people of the intellectual calibre of the apostle Paul?

With regard to (iii), it is possible to imagine various combinations of mistake and deception: for example, a mistake about the identity of the tomb combined with the invention of appearances, or a stealing and secretly disposing of the body combined with hallucinatory appearances, but none seems at all plausible. In fact, alternative (iii) seems even less convincing than (i) or (ii). Would not such a mixture of mistake and deceit have had even less chance of being sustained for long than either the one thing or the other?

---

[12] The suggestion, which has been made, that Jesus was not really dead, but mistaken for dead, and revived in the tomb, does indeed offer a motive for the disciples' deception (to protect Jesus); but otherwise it is exposed to all the objections to alternative (i), and to others besides.

It seems to me that alternative (iv), hard to accept though it undoubtedly is, is the least incredible of the four – by a long way.

The position seems, then, to be that, while the discovery of the dead bones of Jesus would indeed, as C. K. Barrett has rightly maintained,[13] conclusively disprove the church's doctrine of the Resurrection and utterly destroy Christian faith, no amount of scientific, historical-critical or other scholarly activity can prove conclusively that the Resurrection is true. A positive proof of its truth is just not to be had by such means. Certainty with regard to it can come to us only by the work of the Holy Spirit making us free to believe. But it seems to me that the evidence available to us – and I have tried now a good many times to weigh it as carefully and honestly and objectively as I can – is such that, though I cannot prove by historical-critical methods that God raised Jesus from the dead, I can believe it without in any way violating my intellectual or moral integrity. For myself, I must declare that I do indeed confidently believe it.

[13] Barrett, op. cit., p. 349.

12

Some Reflections on the Subject of the Virgin Birth

The affirmation that Jesus Christ 'was conceived by the Holy Ghost, born of the Virgin Mary' is beset by many problems and difficulties, and to deny or try to ignore their existence is bad theological scholarship. But it is also bad theological scholarship – though this is sometimes in danger of being overlooked – to refuse to consider seriously and with as open a mind as possible any evidence or any rational argument, whether historical or theological, which can be adduced as in any way supporting this affirmation of the Apostles' Creed. It seems to me that neither those who accept the historicity of the Virgin Birth nor those who reject it have a monopoly of prejudice. I cannot here attempt anything like a full or systematic discussion of this difficult and controversial subject. The best I can do is to set down briefly and as clearly as I can a few reflections as a very modest contribution to the on-going debate.

I

It is surely right to acknowledge from the start that there is absolutely no possibility of any one's being able to prove the historicity of the Virgin Birth (if it is historical) by historical-critical methods. A positive proof is out of the question. It is also, I think, right to acknowledge that up to the present no proof of its non-historicity has been produced. A good many considerations have indeed been urged, which have seemed to a good many people

*First published in *Scottish Journal of Theology* 41 (1988), pp. 177–89.

to suggest that it is improbable that the Virgin Birth is historical; but a conclusive proof that it is not historical has certainly not been presented. So we are left trying to weigh probabilities; on the evidence available up to date, a conclusive historical–critical decision would seem to be unattainable.

II

An element of quite gratuitous unreality has been introduced into much Christian celebration of Christmas by the tendency to obliterate the distinction between Christmas and Epiphany and bring the wise men into close association with the shepherds. This tendency ignores the facts that, while Luke 2.8 depicts the latter as watching their flocks 'in the same country', Matthew 2.1 and 2 imply that the former had a considerable distance to travel; that, whereas Luke 2.12 and 16 refer to Jesus as a 'babe' (βρέφος: and compare the use of the verb translated 'wrap in swaddling clothes' in vv. 7 and 12), Matthew 2.8, 9, 11, 13, 14 use the word παιδίον (RV: 'young child'), which is appropriate for a child up to six or seven years old; that, whereas the word φάτνη (RV: 'manger') in Luke 2.7, 12, 16 suggests a stable, Matthew 2.11 says that the wise men entered 'into the house'; and that 'from two years old and under' (ἀπὸ διετοῦς καὶ κατωτέρω) in Matthew 2.16 is more plausibly taken as implying that the child whom Herod was determined to make sure of killing was no longer a babe than as an indication of sheer pointless bloodthirstiness. Read carefully, the Infancy Narratives of Matthew and Luke, suggesting as they do an interval of some months between the birth of Jesus and what is related in Matthew 2.1–12, are at least more intelligible than the fictional jumble of much popular Christian imagination. No harm is done by disencumbering the Gospel narratives of extraneous confusion.

III

The main arguments urged against the historicity of the Virgin Birth may now be briefly considered.

1. The paucity of the New Testament attestation of the Virgin Birth is naturally adduced as a strong reason for doubting its historicity. It is indeed directly attested only in Matthew and Luke. But statements to the effect that its New Testament attestation is limited to Matthew and Luke[1] must be firmly challenged. That Paul used γίνεσθαι rather than γεννᾶσθαι in Romans 1.3; Galatians 4.4 and Philippians 2.7 because he knew of the Virgin Birth is, of course, not certain, but it seems to me highly likely.[2] Mark 6.3 is particularly interesting evidence. There is little doubt that ὁ τέκτων, ὁ υἱὸς τῆς Μαρίας should be read.[3] None of the variants (with τοῦ τέκτονος) is likely to be original, for why any of them should have been altered to ὁ τέκτων, ὁ υἱὸς τῆς Μαρίας has never been at all plausibly explained. The alteration could hardly have been made in support of the doctrine of the Virgin Birth, seeing that in the parallels in the two Gospels which explicitly affirm the Virgin Birth Jesus is referred to as 'the carpenter's son' (Matt. 13.55) and 'Joseph's son' (Luke 4.22). If we assume, as we surely must do, that ὁ τέκτων, ὁ υἱὸς τῆς Μαρίας is original in Mark, we have to ask why both the First and Third Evangelists altered it as they did. That they did so because they thought that some Gentile readers might be offended by the idea of Jesus' being a carpenter is scarcely likely. It is much more probable that it was because they recognized the insult conveyed by the metronymic designation. That designation must go back beyond Mark – it cannot plausibly be attributed to his redactional activity – and so is evidence that the charge of illegitimacy, which was certainly levelled against Jesus at a later date, was made very early and quite probably during his

---

[1] So very recently U. Luz, *Das Evangelium nach Matthäus* 1, Zurich, Einsiedeln, Cologne, Neukirchen-Vluyn, 1985, p. 102 ('. . . der im NT nur durch Matthäus und Lukas bezeugten Jungfrauengeburt . . .'). Some systematic theologians have accepted this view of the matter without due questioning (e.g. J. M. Lochman, *The Faith We Confess*, Philadelphia, 1984; Edinburgh, 1986, p. 110).

[2] Cf. the discussion in J. McHugh, *The Mother of Jesus in the New Testament*, London, 1975, pp. 274–7.

[3] It is read by Nestle-Aland[26].

lifetime.[4] It seems likely that John 8.41 reflects both the Fourth Evangelist's knowledge that this charge was current in his time and also his own belief in the virgin birth of Jesus.[5] Two other passages in St John's Gospel very probably allude to the Virgin Birth: 1.13 and 6.41f. With regard to the former, I agree with C. K. Barrett's conclusion that, while the reading which makes an explicit reference to the birth of Jesus should be rejected, 'it remains probable that John was alluding to Jesus' birth, and declaring that the birth of Christians, being bloodless and rooted in God's will alone, followed the pattern of the birth of Christ himself'.[6] With regard to the latter passage too Barrett's judgment seems to me right: it is probable that the evangelist 'knew and accepted the doctrine' of the Virgin Birth and 'that he here ironically alludes to it – if the objectors had known the truth about Jesus' parentage they would have been compelled to recognize that it was entirely congruent with his having come down from heaven'.[7] The paucity of the New Testament evidence for the Virgin Birth is not to be denied, and we shall have something more to say about it in section IV; but what has been said above is enough, I think, to call in question the sweeping assertions which are often made about the silence of the whole New Testament apart from Matthew and Luke.

2. It is sometimes asserted that the very genealogies of Matthew 1 and Luke 3 are themselves witnesses against the historicity of the Virgin Birth, since they would be pointless (so it is said), if Joseph were not the biological father of Jesus, seeing that in them it is through Joseph that his ancestry is traced (Matt. 1.16; Luke 3.23: compare Matt. 1.20; Luke 1.27; 2.4). But the

[4] On Mark 6.3 see further C. E. B. Cranfield, *The Gospel according to St Mark*, Cambridge, ⁹1985, pp. 193–6; E. Stauffer, 'Jeschu ben Mirjam: kontrovers-geschichtliche Anmerkungen zu Mk 6:3', in E. E. Ellis and M. Wilcox (ed.), *Neotestamentica et Semitica: studies in honour of Matthew Black*, Edinburgh, 1969, pp. 119–28.

[5] Cf. C. K. Barrett, *The Gospel according to St John*, London, 2nd edition, 1978, p. 348.

[6] Op. cit., p. 164.

[7] Op. cit., p. 295.

answer to this is surely that Joseph was indeed legally Jesus' father, having made him legally his son by naming him (Matt. 1.25: compare v. 21), and it is in the light of this that Matthew 13.55; Luke 2.33, 41, 43, 48; 4.22 are to be understood. There was clearly a very strong interest in the early church in establishing the Davidic descent of Jesus, in view of the widespread expectation that the Messiah would belong to the family of David, and the significance of the fact that it was in the context of the existence of this strong interest that belief in the virginal conception of Jesus was accepted should not be overlooked.[8]

3. It is argued that the apparent absence of any special understanding of Jesus during his ministry on the part of Mary and her family is inconsonant with the historicity of the Virgin Birth. But, if the birth of Jesus really took place as Matthew and Luke indicate, is it not probable that Mary and Joseph would have been as reticent as possible concerning it in the knowledge that the truth, if revealed, would be likely to attract incredulity and reproach? Moreover, the assumption that, if the doctrine of the Virgin Birth is true, the mother of Jesus herself must for the rest of her life have been immune from all doubt and all misunderstanding of her Son seems to me both psychologically and theologically unsound.

4. Isaiah 7.14 ('Therefore the Lord himself shall give you a sign; behold, a virgin shall conceive, and bear a son, and shall call his name Immanuel') has been claimed to be the origin of the belief in the Virgin Birth. But, in view of the absence of pre-Christian evidence of a messianic interpretation of this passage (it was taken to refer to Hezekiah, the son and successor of Ahaz) and the fact that there is no evidence of its having been understood in pre-Christian Judaism as foretelling a virgin birth, this suggestion is quite improbable. There was nothing in the Hebrew text of the Isaiah verse to suggest a virgin birth, since the word 'almah simply denotes a young woman; and even the Septuagint version would hardly suggest a virginal conception to

[8] See further C. E. B. Cranfield, *A Critical and Exegetical Commentary on the Epistle to the Romans* 1, Edinburgh, [6]1987, pp. 58–9; J. McHugh, op. cit., especially pp. 276–7, 283, 320–1.

any one who had not already got this idea in mind from elsewhere. (More probably the hearer or reader would either understand παρθένος in the sense of 'almah or else take the sentence to mean that one who is at present a virgin will subsequently conceive, not that a virgin will conceive while still a virgin.) But for those who already believed in Jesus' virginal conception, the Septuagint version of Isaiah 7.14 was a most welcome confirmation of their faith.

5. Appeal is made to the existence of a great many alleged parallels: stories of the births of Greek mythological heroes such as Heracles and Perseus and of various historical figures such as Plato, Alexander the Great, Scipio Africanus, Augustus, Apollonius of Tyana; the belief in Egypt that each new king was the offspring of the god Ammon who, assuming the form of the reigning king, had intercourse with the queen; and various other myths and rituals and legends of the ancient Near East and also much farther afield.

It is claimed that, in the light of this wealth of parallel material from the history of religions , acceptance of the historicity of the Virgin Birth is impossible. But none of these alleged parallels is a real parallel. In none of them is there any question of a truly virginal conception: rather is it a matter of physical intercourse between a god and a mortal woman from which a birth results. In fact, the more closely these parallels are examined, the more stark becomes the contrast between them and the narratives of Matthew and Luke. What is attested in the Gospels is a divine act of creation. The fact that early Christian apologetic sometimes appealed to the pagan myths in support of the truth of the Virgin Birth should not be taken to imply that the apologists were unaware of the greatness of the contrast: their appeal was only an *argumentum ad hominem* (those who could accept such stories should not balk at the Virgin Birth).[9]

6. It is argued that much of the rest of the Infancy Narratives is unhistorical and that this suggests doubts about the historicity of the Virginal Conception. I am not going to try to deal with every detail which has been questioned, but shall mention just some

---

[9] See further J. McHugh, op. cit., pp. 290–1.

matters. I hope this will be enough to set a question mark against the academic respectability of the cavalier dismissal of the bulk of Matthew 1 and 2 and Luke 1 and 2 as merely 'unhistorical'.

A cluster of objections concerns the census. Against the statement of Luke 2.1 that 'there went out a decree from Caesar Augustus that all the world should be enrolled' it is objected that there was no census of the whole empire under Augustus. But the fact that under Augustus no census was carried through which embraced every part of the Roman empire at the same time and was completed within a short period does not mean that Luke's statement is without good historical basis. A far-reaching reform of the administration of the empire was certainly carried out under Augustus and it certainly did involve censuses or taxation-assessments of a very thorough and comprehensive kind. Plenty of evidence for them has survived.[10] The work of assessment took varying amounts of time according to the circumstances obtaining in particular areas: it could take several decades. It has been objected that, since at the time of Jesus' birth Judaea was a client state and not part of the empire, a tax-assessment by Augustus' authority could not have taken place there. But a Roman tax-assessment was carried out in the autonomous city-state of Apamea by Quirinius and the fact that towards the end of his life Herod was not in high favour with Rome makes it far from improbable that a Roman tax-assessment was instituted in Judaea.[11] A further objection to Luke's narrative is that Quirinius was governor of Syria from AD 6 to AD 9. There was a census then and it was accompanied by disturbances (compare Acts 5.37). Is the reference to Quirinius, then, in Luke 2.2 an error? Various solutions to the problem have been suggested. The most probable of them would seem to be that favoured by Stauffer, namely, that Quirinius was a commander-in-chief of the east (like Pompey the Great, Marcus Antonius and M. Vipsanius Agrippa) from about 12 BC, sometimes

[10] Cf. E. Stauffer, *Jesus and His Story*, London, 1960, pp. 28–31, 167; N. G. L. Hammond and H. H. Scullard (ed.), *The Oxford Classical Dictionary*, 2nd ed., 1970, p. 220 (s.v. 'Census').
[11] Cf. Stauffer, op. cit., pp. 31–3, 167–8.

governing on his own, sometimes together with an imperial procurator. On this view, Luke 2.1ff will refer to the first stage of the taxation-assessment, and Acts 5.37 to its final stages.[12] Two other objections, that Joseph would not have been required to go to Bethlehem from Nazareth (Luke 2.3–4) and that Mary would not have had to go also (Luke 2.5), are probably mistaken; for, if Joseph had any rights in any property in his ancestral home-town, he would have had to appear there for registration, and, while in a census of Roman citizens only the father of the family was required to appear, it seems clear that in a first assessment in a province or (as here) in a client state women also had to appear.[13]

The account of the visit of the Magi is regarded by many as a product of haggadic imagination; but Stauffer's claim that it 'stands on solid ground'[14] is not easily dismissed. The Berlin Table (of planets) and the Star Almanac of Sippar (on the Euphrates) have shown how accurately astronomers at the end of the first century BC could calculate in advance the orbits and conjunctions of planets. In the year 7 BC the planet Jupiter was involved in a particularly interesting and striking series of events. In the spring it crossed the path of the planet Venus, and in the summer and autumn it met the planet Saturn several times in the rare *conjunctio magna*. It seems perverse to refuse to consider seriously the possibility that the narrative of Matthew 2.1ff rests on a basis of fact and that certain Magi did observe in the place where they lived the beginning[15] of this orbit of Jupiter; that, as a result of their observation and of the astrological significance they attributed to the phenomena which they were able to predict, they set out on an expedition to Palestine; and that, when they were there, they witnessed the climax of these celestial phenomena. It seems to me

---

[12] Stauffer, op. cit., pp. 33–4, 35–6, 168. See also McHugh, op. cit., pp. 141f (he notes that Josephus refers to what is mentioned in Acts 5.37 as an ἀποτίμησις, not an ἀπογραφή).

[13] Cf. Stauffer, op. cit., pp. 34–5, 168.

[14] Op. cit., p. 37.

[15] ἐν τῇ ἀνατολῇ in Matthew 2.2 and 9 is better taken to mean 'at its rising' than 'in the east'.

reasonable to suppose that the basis of what is said about the star in these verses of Matthew is not an imaginary tale of a highly bizarre miracle but a sequence of natural and predictable phenomena, to which at the time, in accordance with contemporary astrological ideas, special political and dynastic significance was attributed.[16]

The historicity of the massacre of the children has also been doubted. Could the story have originated in the desire to bring out the parallel between Jesus and Moses (see Exod. 1.8–2.10)? Is Herod likely to have perpetrated such a crime? Would Augustus have allowed it to pass unpunished? Once again Stauffer makes a case for historicity.[17] His appeal to the evidence of the *Assumption of Moses* 6.2–4 and, in particular, to the words 'and the young' in v. 4 ('He shall slay the old and the young, and he shall not spare') is telling. The passage clearly refers to Herod, and it is to be dated in the period AD 6–30. May it perhaps be very early, independent evidence of the massacre of the innocents? At least, it would be wise not to be too confident in setting down the whole of Matthew 2.13–23 as unhistorical.

One other matter may be mentioned here, namely, the fact that angels are said to play a part. For many that is a sure sign of non-historicity. That angels as generally depicted in Christian art even in its highest reaches are quite incredible is surely to be acknowledged. But, before we also dismiss out of hand the angels as they figure in the biblical testimony, we should, I think, be well advised to pay serious attention to what Barth had to say on the subject in the *Church Dogmatics* III/3, pp. 369 – 519 (= *Kirchliche*

---

[16] See further Stauffer, op. cit., pp. 36–8, 169. With regard to Matthew 2.9, it should surely be said that to insist that the evangelist meant that the star actually travelled in front of the Magi from Jerusalem to Bethlehem at a camel's pace (having already preceded them in this way from their home to Jerusalem) and then came to a sudden stop immediately above the stable is more than a little pedantic and prosaic. (That the Magi themselves, if they were of the calibre of the men who worked in Sippar, are not likely to have entertained any such idea, should go without saying!) Is it not rather like insisting that every one who uses the expressions 'sunrise' and 'sunset' must believe that the sun goes round the earth?

[17] Op. cit., pp. 38–42.

Dogmatik III/3, pp. 426–608).[18] Having read and pondered it, I am not disposed to regard the presence of angels in Matthew 1 and 2 and Luke 1 and 2 as a reason for questioning the historicity of the Virgin Birth.

7. There is yet another argument, one which is not often stated in so many words as an argument against acceptance of the Virgin Birth as historical but which does, I suspect, work powerfully at the back of many people's minds. It is the tacit assumption that miracles do not and cannot happen, and that, since the Virgin Birth would be a miracle, it cannot have occurred. John McHugh is surely right in maintaining that, while an atheist can with logical consistency assert that a virginal conception in impossible, it is not possible for any one who believes in a Creator God or is an agnostic to assert this with logical consistency.[19] A good many Christians, I suspect, have, without being aware of what they were doing, taken over some of the assumptions of an atheistic world-view and allowed them to exercise a veto over their thinking.

IV

There are two considerations, each of which by itself strongly suggests, but which, together, seem to me to make it virtually certain, that Joseph was not biologically the father of Jesus. The first is the fact that on this the otherwise diverse testimonies of two mutually hostile witnesses, the Christian and the Jewish traditions, are agreed, the former asserting that Jesus was born of a virgin, the latter that he was the offspring of Mary and some man other than Joseph.[20] The agreement between mutually opposed witnesses has, other things being equal, to be accorded special respect. By itself,

18 A stimulating brief account of these pages of Barth is W. A. Whitehouse, 'God's heavenly kingdom and His servants the angels', in *SJT* 4 (1951), pp. 376–82, reprinted in his *The Authority of Grace: essays in response to Karl Barth*, Edinburgh, 1981, pp. 47–52.

19 Op. cit., p. 322.

20 Cf. Stauffer, op cit., pp. 23–5, 165f; also the essay by him cited above. See also H. Chadwick, *Origen: Contra Celsum*, Cambridge, ³1980, p. 31, n. 3.

however, this consideration does not prove the point, since it does not exclude the possibility that the Christian claim was the creation of some doctrinal, apologètic or other interest (and that the Jewish reproach was a response to the Christian claim) or the possibility that the Jewish reproach was a slander without any foundation whatsoever and the Christian claim a reaction to it. When, however, the second consideration is joined to the first, those possibilities are ruled out. This second consideration is the recognition of the significance of four facts in combination, namely:

(i) that the earliest church was firmly convinced that Jesus was the Messiah;

(ii) that there was no pre-Christian expectation that the Messiah would be virgin-born;

(iii) that there was a very strong – even if not quite universal – expectation that the Messiah would be a descendant of David;

(iv) that the Davidic descent of Joseph was affirmed.

(These four facts in combination surely do make it virtually impossible to suppose that Christians could have simply invented the Virgin Birth, whether on their own initiative or as a reply to a Jewish slander, knowing all the time that Jesus was Joseph's son by Mary.) Taken together, these two considerations seem to me to compel us to regard the view that Jesus was the offspring of the union of Joseph and Mary as a non-starter and to accept it as virtually certain that we have only two alternatives from which to choose: either Jesus was the son of Mary and of some man other than Joseph, or the affirmation of the Virgin Birth is true.

While it is clear that there is no question of our being able to arrive at a choice between these two alternatives which is absolutely certain from a historical-critical point of view, there are, I think, some things which can be said with considerable confidence. It can, for one thing, be said that it is vastly more difficult to explain how the early church came to believe in the Virgin Birth, if it is unhistorical, than many recent New Testament scholars have assumed. The inadequacy of the alleged parallels as an explanation becomes more and more apparent, the more closely one examines them. The question has to be asked, whether the confident appeal to, and accumulation of, parallels has not been marked by a degree of superficiality and lack of discrimination. This question was raised for me acutely, when I read recently in the first volume of Luz's commentary on Matthew (which seems to me to be in many ways an outstandingly fresh, stimulating and well written contribution to Matthean studies) the astonishing assertion that the evidence for the miraculous birth of Plato is superior to the evidence for the virgin birth of Jesus.[21] The multiplication of pseudo-parallels does not help; for, if these 'parallels' are not real parallels, a hundred of them or a thousand count for no more than one, since – something which, in this connection, New Testament scholars have tended to forget – the value of nought multiplied by a hundred or by a thousand, like that of nought multiplied by one, is precisely nought. Up to the present no tolerably credible explanation of how belief in the Virgin Birth arose, if the Virgin Birth is not historical, has been forthcoming.

But those alleged parallels may indeed have an important bearing on the most significant of the arguments advanced against the historicity of the Virgin Birth, namely, the paucity of its New Testament attestation. For, while they are not close enough substantially for it to be at all plausible to suppose them to have been the source of the Christian belief in the Virgin Birth, they are superficially close enough to have been a powerful reason for the church's reticence about it. The church may well have sensed the danger that the Virgin Birth, if proclaimed in the Gentile world, would be misunderstood along the lines of the pagan myths, as being like the birth of a Perseus or a Heracles, or as a mere flattering fancy like the stories of the births of Plato, Alexander, Augustus. Such a fear may well have been an important reason for the church's reticence and so for the paucity of New Testament

[21] Luz, op cit., p. 102, n. 25. But how can one believe that Diogenes Laertius 3.2 warrants the assertion, 'Die Quellenlage ist hier [i.e. with regard to the supernatural birth of Plato] besser als bei Jesus'? Other references (not specified by Luz) for the story of Plato's birth are given by Chadwick, op. cit., p. 321, n. 12. Origen's own reference in *Contra Celsum* 1.37 should also be mentioned.

attestation. But, when once the doctrine had come to be widely known outside the church, apologists would, not unnaturally, use the *ad hominem* argument that those who could believe the pagan stories had no reason to balk at the Virgin Birth.[22]

In the earliest period, the lifetime of Jesus himself, it is surely understandable that, if the Virgin Birth is historical, Mary and Joseph should have been reticent about it, trying very hard to keep the strange circumstances of Jesus' birth unknown to family and neighbours. They may have done this partly out of reverence for God's action. But they certainly had a very obvious and over-whelming reason for trying to keep their secret to themselves in the knowledge that its disclosure would be bound to be met by incredulity and reproaches. The conclusion that Mary had done wrong would naturally be drawn.

That the secret would somehow get out and rumours begin to circulate is also understandable. That they were already circulating during the lifetime of Jesus seems highly probable.

It is, surely, extremely difficult, on the assumption that the Virgin Birth is not historical, to explain at all convincingly how the early church came during the first century to affirm it, in spite of the fact that there was no expectation that the Messiah would be virgin-born, in spite of the certainty that such an affirmation would be met by incredulity and ridicule among Jews, in spite of the church's own interest in maintaining the Davidic descent of Jesus, and in spite of the obvious danger that among Gentiles the doctrine would be misunderstood along the lines of pagan mythology. The arguments for rejecting the historicity of the Virgin Birth seem to me, as I examine them yet again, not nearly as strong as they are often assumed to be, and the arguments for accepting it seem to me weighty. I have to declare myself convinced that I can, without violating my intellectual integrity, affirm with the Apostles' Creed, *ex animo*, without mental reservations and without shuffling, that Jesus Christ 'was conceived by the Holy Ghost, born of the Virgin Mary'. I also recognize that I have to be willing to undertake again and again the task of careful consideration of the relevant evidence,

---

[22] Cf. McHugh, op. cit., pp. 290f.

if fresh possibly relevant material is brought to light or someone else's re-examination of the evidence (with a different conclusion) seems sufficiently thorough and competent to demand it.

V

In conclusion, I must give but the barest hint of what I take to be the theological significance of the Virgin Birth.

(i) It does not prove the truth of the Incarnation. And we may not say that God could not have effected the Incarnation otherwise than in this way. But the way in which, according to the New Testament and the Creeds, he did effect it is profoundly eloquent. The Virgin Birth points to the *mystery* of the personal union of God and man in Jesus Christ.

(ii) The statement in the Creed that Jesus Christ 'was conceived by the Holy Ghost' (compare Matt. 1.18, 20; Luke 1.35) indicates that God himself made a new beginning in the course of the history of his creation by coming himself in person and becoming part of that history. He himself originated this particular human life by a new act of creation. Jesus Christ is not a saviour arising out of the continuity of our human history, but God in person intervening in it, coming to the rescue.

(iii) He was 'born of . . . Mary'. He is truly human. The Word really did become flesh, that is, assume our nature, become true man, while still remaining what he always was.

(iv) The Virginal Conception attests the fact that God's redemption of his creation was by grace alone. The *sola* of *sola gratia* is seriously meant and must be seriously acknowledged. Our humanity, represented by Mary, here does nothing more than just accept – and even that acceptance is God's gracious gift. That is the real significance of the κεχαριτωμένη of Luke 1.28. Our fallen humanity's rôle is here strictly limited. The male sex, which has been characteristically the dominant, powerful, aggressive element of humanity, is altogether excluded from this action (and must we not see as included in this exclusion all dominant, powerful, aggressive manifestations of female *homo sapiens* as well?), and our pride and self-reliant initiative set aside, our humanity's part is here simply to be made the receptacle of God's gift, to be enabled to submit to be the object of God's mercy: *Ecce ancilla Domini: fiat mihi secundum verbum tuum.*[23]

---

[23] On the significance of the Virgin Birth reference should be made to Barth's *Church Dogmatics* I/2, pp. 172–202 (= *Kirchliche Dogmatik* I/2, pp. 187–221); also *Dogmatics in Outline*, London, 1949, pp. 95–100 (a magnificent six pages which deserve and require to be read and re-read with very great attentiveness); and J. McHugh, op. cit., pp. 330–42.

13

A Response to
Professor Richard B. Hays'
The Moral Vision of the New Testament

The Moral Vision of the New Testament[1] is undoubtedly a very important book. It is not surprising that it has been received with widespread and enthusiastic acclaim. It has many admirable qualities. Its structure is well thought out and satisfying. It is clearly and attractively written and will be readily intelligible to others besides New Testament specialists. The author's sincerity is palpable, his Christian commitment obvious, his learning impressive. The fact that he has wrestled earnestly with some of the moral problems which confront the church at the end of the twentieth century and the beginning of the twenty-first is everywhere apparent. I for one read his book with unflagging interest and found it difficult to put down. Professor Hays is to be congratulated on having produced a fine and exhilarating book. He has put not only New Testament scholars and all who specialize in Christian ethics but also the church at large in his debt. It is because the book is so valuable and likely to be very influential that it is, I think, important to note some of its weaknesses.

Hays says on p. 3: 'Unless we can give a coherent account of our methods for moving between text and normative ethical

[1] *The Moral Vision of the New Testament: Community, Cross, New Creation: A Contemporary Introduction to New Testament Ethics*, New York, 1996; Edinburgh, 1997.

judgments, appeals to the authority of Scripture will be hollow and unconvincing. It is my aim in this book, therefore, to articulate as clearly as possible a framework within which we might pursue New Testament ethics as a normative theological discipline: the goal of the inquiry will be to clarify how the church can read Scripture in a faithful and disciplined manner so that Scripture might come to shape the life of the church.' The great care with which he has striven to establish a credible method of moving from the text to its application to the life of the church is a valuable feature of his book.

The work consists of four parts. Part I is entitled 'The Descriptive Task', and gives summary accounts of the moral visions of the major New Testament witnesses. Part II ('The Synthetic Task') is concerned with the question whether it is possible to discern among the diverse voices and apparent tensions a unity of ethical perspective. Here Hays argues that we have to identify certain key images which all the canonical writings share. He proposes three: community, cross, new creation. These, he suggests, 'can focus and guide our reading of the New Testament texts with respect to ethical issues' (p. 198), serving as '*lenses* that bring our reading of the canonical texts into sharper focus as we seek to discern what is central and fundamental in the ethical vision of the New Testament as a whole' (p. 200). Part III ('The Hermeneutical Task') is concerned with the use of the New Testament in Christian ethics. Its central chapter is a discussion of five representative theologians' hermeneutical strategies. This is preceded and followed by useful chapters aimed at the clarification and refinement of hermeneutical procedures. Part IV ('The Pragmatic Task') deals with five test cases: violence in defence of justice; divorce and remarriage; homosexuality; anti-Judaism and ethnic conflict; and abortion. These five issues, the author tells us in his Conclusion, were chosen for methodological rather than substantive reasons and do not fully reflect his judgment as to what are the most pressing issues facing the church today – though, of the four 'fundamental issues' listed on p. 463 as demanding our energy and attention today, two have in fact been considered as the first and the fourth of the five test cases, another, 'the unity of men and women', has been touched on in connection with the second test case and the remaining one, 'the sharing of possessions', is discussed briefly in the Conclusion.

My first complaint against *The Moral Vision of the New Testament* is that, as far as I can see, its author has not attempted a serious exegesis of those New Testament passages which seem to indicate that the Christian has an obligation to the civil authority. The clearest and most emphatic of them is, of course, Romans 13.1–7, every verse of which calls for careful exegesis. But alongside it must be placed Mark 12.13–17 (= Matt. 22.15–22; Luke 20.20–26); 1 Timothy 2.1–7; Titus 3.1–2; 1 Peter 2.13–17. In addition we should consider the implications of the accounts of Paul's use of his Roman citizenship in Acts 16.37–39; 22.25–29, and of his appeal to Caesar in Acts 25.8–12. A careful study of all these passages is enough, I believe, to establish that there is widespread agreement among the New Testament writers that the Christian has a duty to the state. (That Revelation stands apart from the rest of the New Testament in its view of the Roman empire is obvious. Written most probably towards the end of the principate of Domitian, who insisted on being addressed by his officials as 'our Lord and God' and whose last years were something of a 'Terror', it is a powerful warning that the relatively just state can degenerate only too easily into a monster of injustice.)

In the circumstances of the Roman empire, an authoritarian state, the duty owed was limited. I have suggested elsewhere that, on the basis of the passages which bear on the subject, we may list the following things as included: showing respect to the emperor and his representatives (Rom. 13.7; 1 Pet. 2.17); paying taxes (Mark 12.13ff and parallels; Rom. 13.6f); obedience in so far as it does not conflict with obedience to God (Tit. 3.1); a serious and responsible disobedience whenever to obey would involve disobeying God; prayer for the authorities (1 Tim. 2.1ff); and witness to Christ in their presence (Mark 13.9).[2]

---

[2] 'The Christian's Political Responsibility according to the New Testament', in C. E. B. Cranfield, *The Bible and Christian Life*, Edinburgh, 1985, pp. 48–68. For an exegesis of Romans 13.1–7 I may refer to my *A Critical and Exegetical Commentary on the Epistle to the Romans* 2, Edinburgh, ⁵1989, pp. 651–73.

If I am right in thinking that there is no reason to believe that a democratic form of state is less acceptable to God than an autocratic, then surely those Christians who live in democracies must try to work out what in their situation is the equivalent to the being subject to the governing authorities, which St Paul enjoins in Romans 13.1, 5. I take it that the basic idea expressed by the Greek verb ὑποτάσσεσθαι with the dative in Romans 13.1 is 'to allow the claim someone has on one to take priority over the claim one has on oneself'. The Christian who lives in a democracy then, if he would be obedient to the New Testament teaching, must put the true well-being of the state of which he is a citizen before his own interests, in the knowledge that its existence is a part of God's merciful provision for the good of human beings. He will recognize that his democratic state needs much more from him than the Roman empire needed from its inhabitants and that he can – and therefore surely must – do much more towards the maintenance of the state as a just state than was ever possible for them. He will recognize that, in addition to fulfilling those obligations to the state which are actually specified in the New Testament, he must also try conscientiously to do to the best of his ability those extra things which a democratic state needs from its citizens, if it is to function properly as a democratic state. These include at any rate responsible participation in elections both national and local; a serious and sustained endeavour to keep oneself as fully and reliably informed as possible about political issues, since responsible voting is possible only on the basis of adequate knowledge; criticism of the government, its policies and its implementation of them, in the light of the gospel and law of God; and an unceasing endeavour to support just and humane policies and to oppose those policies and particular decisions which are unjust or inhumane by the various means which are constitutionally open to one. Must we not accept that for us to fail to try seriously to render these services to the state to which we belong would be to refuse to be subject to the authority (ἀντιτάσσεσθαι τῇ ἐξουσίᾳ) and so to oppose God's ordering and bring upon ourselves God's judgment (Rom. 13.2)?

To omit to address the issue of the Christian's political responsibility in a book on the ethical vision of the New Testament seems to me a very serious omission.

My second criticism is more tentative. I cannot help wondering whether Professor Hays' three 'images' (community, cross, new creation) are enough. Two other 'images' seem to me to have a strong claim to be considered. The first of them is 'creation'. Is not the fact that the God revealed in Jesus is the Creator a matter of very great importance for the New Testament writers? Is not faith in God as Creator and also the Sustainer and Ruler of his creation the context in which Professor Hays' three images function? Its bearing on ethics may be seen in Romans 1.18–32 but also in such passages as Matthew 6.25–34; 10.29f; 1 Peter 4.19. Does not Professor Hays' omission of creation from his list of 'images' have the effect of obscuring the fact that God elected a community not just for its own sake but for the sake of his whole creation, because he was and is and always will be the 'faithful Creator' (1 Pet. 4.19), faithful to all that he has created? Was not John Calvin being true to the New Testament, when in discussing the words 'Our Father' in the Lord's Prayer he insisted that the Christian should in his prayers 'embrace all who are his brothers in Christ, not only those whom he at present sees and recognizes as such but all men [= *homines*, i.e. human beings] who dwell on earth'?[3]

The second possible extra 'image' is 'Jesus is Lord' or 'Christ exalted'. Romans 10.9; 1 Corinthians 12.3; 2 Corinthians 4.5; Philippians 2.11 are evidence for the early use of 'Jesus is Lord' (κύριος Ἰησοῦς) as a confessional formula in the church, and this, together with the number of times that Psalm 110.1 is quoted or echoed in the New Testament, suggests that the focal point of the early church's faith was the present reign of the exalted Christ. (When Paul says that he preaches 'Christ crucified' (1 Cor. 1.23; 2.2), he most certainly wants to emphasize the never-ending importance of the cross; but he does not mean that he preaches Christ crucified as though he were still on the cross. The cross is

---

[3] *Institutes of the Christian Religion*, translated by F. L. Battles, London, 1961, 2, p. 901.

significant because it was not the end. At the same time Christ's lordship is only truly understood in the light of the cross. The object of the preaching is the exalted crucified one.) We may compare Matthew 28.18; John 17.2; Ephesians 1.20–23; 1 Peter 3.22; Revelation 1.5; 17.14; 19.16. If I am right in my understanding of the affirmation that Jesus is Lord (that it was ascribing to the exalted Jesus the authority and lordship of God himself), then it has an important bearing on the way we think about our political responsibility, since it means that political affairs no less than the life of the church are within the dominion of Christ. When the Christian moves beyond the church's boundaries, he is not passing into the dominion of some other lord, but merely from that sphere in which Christ's lordship is more or less adequately known and more or less sincerely acknowledged into a sphere in which, though, it is not yet known and acknowledged, it is no less real and inescapable.

A third criticism concerns the way in which appeal is made to the example of Jesus. That he is indeed, according to the New Testament, the great example for Christians is certainly not disputed. My worry is that Professor Hays does not seem to take sufficient account of the differences between the situation of Jesus and our situation. Two very significant differences ought surely to be allowed for.

The first is that the New Testament represents Jesus as conscious of having been sent by God expressly 'to give his life a ransom for many'. Death at the hands of men, but by God's appointment, and as the means of delivering human beings, was something he accepted as a necessary part of his mission (e.g. Mark 8.31; 9.31; 10.33–34, 45; 12.6–7, 12; 14.22–24, 35–36; cf. Rom. 5.8, Gal. 2.20; Phil. 2.8). This is not our situation. Our part is to bear witness to Christ bravely (which may indeed be exceedingly costly), not to be co-redeemers.

The second significant difference is that, whether in Galilee which was governed by the tetrarch Herod Antipas, a puppet ruler dependent on Rome, or in Judaea, which had been under direct Roman rule since AD 6, Jesus lived and fulfilled his ministry under an autocratic government and was quite without political power,

172

whereas nationals of the United States of America at the turn of the twentieth century are the privileged citizens of a state, which is not only the richest, most powerful, most influential state on earth, but also a democracy. For them it is possible to exercise very considerable political power either in support of justice and humaneness and in opposition to injustice, inhumanity and oppression, or else – whether by actions or by inaction – to strengthen injustice, inhumanity and oppression, and to frustrate justice and humaneness, not only in their own country but also in many other countries over which their government and their great companies exert great influence. What is true of Christians in the United States is also true, though in a much smaller way, of Christians in Britain and other democracies. While Jesus lived his life 'outside the circle of power',[4] Christians in the United States and in Britain are quite clearly within that circle. In view of this enormous difference between Jesus' situation and ours, it is surely of the greatest importance for us to recognize that there is a real danger that by trying in a wooden way to follow his example we may actually fail to be obedient to him.

I turn now to Professor Hays' discussion of the first of his 'test cases' ('Violence in Defence of Justice'). That war is a terrible, hideous evil, there is absolutely no doubt. To take part in killing one's fellow human beings, whatever the circumstances, is a terrible, hideous thing. The question whether in obedience to Christ the Christian must in all circumstances refuse to take part in it or whether there may be some circumstances in which to refuse to take part in it would be an even greater evil than to fight and kill, is a serious question which has caused many of us much anguish. The answer of the New Testament is not, I think, as clear as Professor Hays would have us believe (he has no doubt that it supports the pacifist position). In any case, we need to be aware of the danger of allowing ourselves to be so preoccupied with trying to decide once for all the question at issue between pacifist and non-pacifist Christians that we fail altogether to give serious attention to the causes of wars. There is surely an urgent need to

---

[4] The phrase is used by Hays, p. 325.

consider in the light of the New Testament such things as long-standing injustices between and within nations, rivalry between ideologies, competition for natural resources and for markets, the frightening power of multinational corporations, the unchecked movement of capital, the pressures exerted by shareholders for ever-increasing dividends, the crippling burdens of third world debt, the pressures of population growth, the insatiable consumption of limited global natural resources by the richest countries, the desperate poverty and hunger of millions, the greed of individuals for power and dominance, and the part played by fear.

If we are unconvinced by the pacifist's contention that the New Testament simply forbids us to take part in, or support, the use of force in any circumstances, we may well decide that the United Nations, for all its faults and failures, represents the best opportunity in our generation for promoting peace and is something which Christians ought to welcome as a gift of God's mercy and try their best to support. That it has often proved weak and ineffective is true; but it is not the project itself that has been shown to be defective, but the will of the various national governments to fulfil their obligations to it. As a forum in which poor and weak countries have a voice as well as the rich and strong, the United Nations General Assembly deserves the respectful attention of Christians. If we are serious in our desire to heed the moral vision of the New Testament, we shall, I believe, do our utmost to persuade our governments to try to make the United Nations more effective, loyally to fulfil their financial and other obligations to it, and to stop seeking to manipulate it for the promotion of their own interests; and we shall surely pray earnestly for God's blessing upon it.

I conclude by making just one more point. With regard to Professor Hays' fourth test case ('Anti-Judaism and Ethnic Conflict'), while I fully share his sense of deep shame at the cruelties inflicted by Christians on Jews in the past, his abhorrence of all anti-Judaism[5] and of all other racial prejudice, and also his

---

[5] Though, in this connection, I would want to question whether on pp. 422–8 and 432–4 Hays is fair to Matthew and John.

eagerness for brotherly dialogue between Christians and Jews, there is one aspect of his discussion that troubles me. It seems to me that there is something wrong in writing about relations between Christians and Jews at the present time without referring to the problem of Israel's treatment of the Palestinian people. Christians are liable to let their proper sense of shame about the sufferings of Jews at the hands of the Nazis render them uncritical of the state of Israel. But we cannot make amends at the Palestinian people's cost for our churches' and our countries' failures to do what could have been done to save Jews in the 1930s and early 1940s. A recent letter from the charity Medical Aid for Palestinians (dated 1 April 1997) speaks of the 'up to 500,000 Palestinian refugees confined to just 22 refugee camps [in Lebanon]', and says that, though a great many of them 'have existed as refugees since 1948, there still remains no prospect of Israel allowing them to exercise the right of returning to their homes in cities such as Haifa and Jaffa'. It goes on to describe conditions: 'Many of the camps do not have even basic amenities. There is chronic overcrowding, open drainage of sewage, limited water supplies, malnutrition, and little or no access to basic health care.' But what is happening in the refugee camps in Lebanon is only one bit of the wrong that is being done to the Palestinian people. We read in our newspapers of Mr Netanyahu's cavalier treatment of the Oslo Agreement and his insistence on continuing to build more and more Jewish settlements in a cynical attempt to frustrate the peace agreement by more and more concrete 'facts on the ground'. For Christians to be blind to the wrongs which are being perpetrated against the Palestinians every day by Israel is not the right way to seek reconciliation between Christians and Jews. For us to fail now to speak out clearly and persistently against what Israel is doing would be a grievous betrayal of those Jews both outside and within Israel who have courageously opposed the Israeli government's actions and also, I believe, the cruellest injury which we could possibly inflict on the Jewish people as a whole.

List of the Author's Publications Excluding Reviews

(those republished in *The Bible and Christian Life*, 1985, are marked by an asterisk, those republished in the present volume by two asterisks)

1941

'Look before you leap', in *Community* (1940–41), pp. 44–5.

'"... but ... therefore ..." or signposts in the Epistle to the Romans', in *The Student Movement* 44 (1941–42), pp. 22–3.

1942

'The Church and Belshazzar: a study in the fifth chapter of Daniel', in *The Student Movement* 44 (1941–42), pp. 107–8.

'Grace: a meditation upon Psalm 90', in *The Student Movement* 45 (1942–43), pp. 13–14.

1943

* 'An interpretation of the Book of Job', in *The Expository Times* 54 (1942–43), pp. 295–8.

1944

'The burden which Habakkuk the prophet did see', in *The Student Movement* 46 (1943–44), pp. 119–20.

1945

'The Vision of the Divine Warrior (Isa. 63.1–6)', in *The Student Movement* 47 (1944–45), pp. 67–8.

1948

'The cup metaphor in Mark 14.36 and parallels', in *The Expository Times* 59 (1947–48), pp. 137–8.

1949

'The love of God', in *The Student Movement* 51 (1948–49), no. 3, pp. 6–9.

1950

The First Epistle of Peter, London, 1950; 4th impression, 1958.

'St Mark 9.14–29', in *Scottish Journal of Theology* 3 (1950), pp. 57–67.

'Fellowship', 'Love', etc. in A. Richardson (ed.), *A Theological Word Book of the Bible*, London, 1950.

1951

'Riches and the kingdom of God: Mark 10.17–31', in *Scottish Journal of Theology* 4 (1951), pp. 302–13.

'St Mark 4.1–34: Part I', in *Scottish Journal of Theology* 4 (1951), pp. 398–414.

1952

'St Mark 4.1–34: Part II', in *Scottish Journal of Theology* 5 (1952), pp. 49–66.

'The first recorded Christian service? (Luke 24.13–35)', in *The Student Movement* 54 (1951–52), no. 4, pp. 11–13.

'A pastor's thanksgiving and intercession for a local church (Phil. 1.3–11)', in *The Student Movement* 54 (1951–52), no. 5, pp. 10–13.

'St Mark 16.1–8: Part I' and 'St Mark 16.1–8: Part II', in *Scottish Journal of Theology* 5 (1952), pp. 282–98 and 398–414.

1953

'St Mark 13', in *Scottish Journal of Theology* 6 (1953), pp. 189–96 and 287–303.

1954

'St Mark 13' (continued), in *Scottish Journal of Theology* 7 (1954), pp. 284–303.

'The Good Samaritan (Luke 10.25–37)', in *Theology Today* 11 (1954), pp. 368–72; reprinted, with slight alterations, in *The Service of God* (see under 1965) and in *If God be for us*, 1985.

'Romans 7 reconsidered', in *The Expository Times* 65 (1953–54), p. 221.

1955

'Message of hope: Mark 4.21–32', in *Interpretation* 9 (1955), pp. 150–64.

'The baptism of our Lord – a study of St Mark 1.9–11', in *Scottish Journal of Theology* 8 (1955), pp. 53–63.

'St John' and '1 Peter', in G. H. Davies and A. Richardson (ed.), *The Teachers' Commentary*, revised ed., London, 1955, pp. 439–50 and 504–10.

'St Matthew 25.31–46', in *The Presbyterian Messenger* 110 (1955), no. 1252, pp. 2–3.

1956

'The witness of the New Testament to Christ', in T. H. L. Parker (ed.), *Essays in Christology for Karl Barth* (London, 1956), pp. 71–91.

'Jesus Christ is Lord', in *The Presbyterian Messenger* 111 (1956), no. 1265, pp. 2–3.

1957

The Epistle of James: four studies (a brief study outline published by the Student Christian Movement), London, 1957.

1958

* 'The interpretation of 1 Peter 3.19 and 4.6', in *The Expository Times* 69 (1957–58), pp. 369–72.

* 'Divine and human action: the biblical concept of worship', in *Interpretation* 12 (1958), pp. 387–98; reprinted, with slight alterations and an additional note, in *The Service of God* (see under 1965).

1959

The Gospel according to Saint Mark (Cambridge Greek Testament Commentary), Cambridge, 1959. Reprinted with supplementary notes, 1963; with additional supplementary notes, 1966; with further revision in subsequent impressions; 11th impression 1994.

1960

'Some observations on Romans 13.1–7', in *New Testament Studies* 6 (1959–60), pp. 241–9.

I and II Peter and Jude (Torch Bible Commentaries), London, 1960.

1961

'Diakonia (Matthew 25.31–46', in *The London Quarterly and Holborn Review* 186 (1961), pp. 275–81; reprinted in *The Service of God* (see under 1965) and in *If God be for us*, 1985.

1962

* 'The Christian's political responsibility according to the New Testament', in *Scottish Journal of Theology* 15 (1962), pp. 176–92; reprinted in *The Service of God* (see under 1965). A Spanish translation was published in C. E. B. Cranfield and A. Skevington Wood. *Responsabilidad Social y politica*, Buenos Aires, 1972. The article was republished in *Metanoia* 3 (1993), pp. 16–28, and in *Reformed Review* 50 (1996), pp. 5–18.

* Μέτϱον πίστεως in Romans 12.3', in *New Testament Studies* 8 (1961–62), pp. 345–51.

Commentary on 1 Peter and general article on the Catholic Epistles, in M. Black and H. H. Rowley (ed.), *Peake's Commentary on the Bible*, 1962.

'Mark, Gospel of' in G. A. Buttrick (ed.), *The Interpreter's Dictionary of the Bible*. New York and Nashville, 1962, vol. 3, pp. 267–77.

Brief articles in B. Reicke and L. Rost (ed.), *Biblisch-Historisches Handwörterbuch* 1, Göttingen, 1962.

1963

A Ransom for Many, London. 1963; reprinted in *If God be for us*, 1985.

'The Parable of the Unjust Judge and the eschatology of Luke–Acts', in *Scottish Journal of Theology* 16 (1963), pp. 297–301.

1964

'St Paul and the law', in *Scottish Journal of Theology* 17 (1964), pp. 43–68; reprinted in R. Batey (ed.), *New Testament Issues*, New York and Evanston, 1970.

'The Gospel in action: St Luke 14.12–14', in R. J. W. Bevan (ed.), *The Christian Way Explained: sermons on belief and behaviour by the Archbishop of York: and other preachers*. London, 1964, pp. 49–56; reprinted in *If God be for us*, 1985.

* 'The significance of διὰ παντός in Romans 11.10', in F. L. Cross (ed.), *Studia Evangelica* II, part 1, Berlin, 1964, pp. 546–50.

Brief articles in B. Reicke and L. Rost (ed.), *Biblisch-Historisches Handwörterbuch* 2, Göttingen, 1964.

1965

A Commentary on Romans 12–13 (*Scottish Journal of Theology*, Occasional Papers 12), Edinburgh, 1965.

The Service of God, London, 1965.

'Minister and congregation in the light of 2 Corinthians 4.5–7: an exposition', in *Interpretation* 19 (1965), pp. 163–7.

* 'The message of James', in *Scottish Journal of Theology* 18 (1965), pp. 182–93 and 338–45.

1966

'Romans 8.28', in *Scottish Journal of Theology* 19 (1966), pp. 204–15.

* 'Diakonia in the New Testament', in J. I. McCord and T. H. L. Parker (ed.), *Service in Christ: essays presented to Karl Barth on his 80th birthday*, London, 1966, pp. 37–48.

Brief articles in B. Reicke and L. Rost (ed.), *Biblisch-Historiches Handwörterbuch* 3, Göttingen, 1966.

1967

* 'New church constitutions and diakonia', in *Scottish Journal of Theology* 20 (1967), pp. 338–41.

* 'Hebrews 13.20–1', in *Scottish Journal of Theology* 20 (1967), pp. 437–41.

'What is the Gospel?', in *Outlook* (official magazine of the Presbyterian Church of England) 1 (1967), no. 4, p. 10.

1968

'Romans 1.18', in *Scottish Journal of Theology* 21 (1968), pp. 330–5.

'Are annotated Bibles desirable?', in *The Churchman* 82 (1968), pp. 290–6.

1969

'A reply to Mr. Bradnock', in *The Churchman* 83 (1969), pp. 28–30. Postscript on section headings for Bibles', in *The Churchman* 83 (1969), pp. 203–5.

'On some of the problems in the interpretation of Romans 5.12', in *Scottish Journal of Theology* 22 (1969), pp. 324–41.

'True religion: a sermon on Micah 6.8', in *Communio Viatorum* 12 (1969), pp. 191–5; reprinted in *If God be for us*, 1985.

1972

'"You" or "Thou"' (letter to the editor), in *Outlook* 6 (1972), no. 54, p. 18.

'You and Thou' (letter to the editor), in *Outlook* 6 (1972), no. 56, p. 23.

1974

* 'Some observations on Romans 8.19–21', in R. Banks (ed.), *Reconciliation and Hope: New Testament essays on atonement and eschatology presented to L. L. Morris on his 60th birthday*, Exeter, 1974, pp. 224–30.

'The freedom of the Christian according to Romans 8.2', in M. E. Glasswell and E. W. Fasholé-Luke (ed.), *New Testament Christianity for Africa and the World: essays in honour of Harry Sawyerr*, London, 1974, pp. 91–8.

'Some observations on the interpretation of Romans 14.1–15.13', in *Communio Viatorum* 17 (1974), pp. 193–204.

1975

* 'The preacher and his authority', in *Epworth Review* 2 (1975), pp. 95–106.

'Some notes on Romans 9.30–33', in E. E. Ellis and E. Grässer (ed.), *Jesus und Paulus: Festschrift für Werner Georg Kümmel zum 70. Geburtstag*, Göttingen, 1975, pp 35–43.

A Critical and Exegetical Commentary on the Epistle to the Romans 1 (The International Critical Commentary), Edinburgh, 1975; with numerous corrections in subsequent impressions; 9th impression 1998. A Korean translation of this together with volume 2 was published, Seoul, 1994; a Chinese translation of this volume was published, Taipei, 1997.

1978

'A comment on Mark 10.1–12 on marriage and the remarriage of divorced people', in a collection of papers, *Marriage, Divorce and Remarriage*, United Reformed Church, 1978.

1979

A Critical and Exegetical Commentary on the Epistle to the Romans 2, Edinburgh, 1979; with numerous corrections in subsequent impressions; 6th impression 1994.

* 'A study of 1 Thessalonians 2', in *Irish Biblical Studies* 1 (1979), pp. 215–26.

1980

'Romans 9.30–10.4', in *Interpretation* 34 (1980), pp. 70–4.

1981

Sermon on Matthew 11.28–30, in *Kingsmen* 35 (Spring term 1981), pp. 25–9; reprinted in *If God be for us*, 1985.

1982

* 'Light from St Paul on Christian-Jewish relations', in D. W. Torrance (ed.), *The Witness of the Jews to God*, Edinburgh, 1982, pp. 23–31.

'John 1.14: "became"', in *The Expository Times* 93 (1981–82), p. 215.

* 'Changes of person and number in Paul's Epistles', in M. D. Hooker and S. G. Wilson (ed.), *Paul and Paulinism: essays in honour of C. K. Barrett*, London, 1982, pp. 280–9.

* 'Thoughts on New Testament eschatology', in *Scottish Journal of Theology* 35 (1982), pp. 497–512.

1983

'Some questions evoked by *Baptism, Eucharist and Ministry*', in *Focus on Unity* (the newsletter of the Ecumenical Response Group in the United Reformed Church), no. 3 (1983), pp. 6–7.

1985

Romans: a shorter commentary, Edinburgh and Grand Rapids, 1985; 5th impression 1995. A Portuguese translation was published, São Paulo, 1992; a Spanish translation, Buenos Aires and Grand Rapids, 1993; and a Korean translation, Seoul, 1997.

If God be for us: a collection of sermons, Edinburgh, 1985.

The Bible and Christian Life: a collection of essays, Edinburgh, 1985.

1986

'The interpretation of Romans 9–11', in A. P. F. Sell (ed.), *Reformed Theology and the Jewish People*, Geneva, 1986, pp. 55–63.

1987

** 'Some comments on Professor J. D. G. Dunn's *Christology in the Making*, with special reference to the evidence of the Epistle to the Romans', in L. D. Hurst and N. T. Wright (ed.), *The Glory of Christ in the New Testament: studies in Christology in memory of G. B. Caird*, Oxford, 1987, pp. 267–80.

** 'Preaching on Romans', in *The Expository Times* 99 (1987–88), pp. 36–40.

1988

** 'Some reflections on the subject of the Virgin Birth', in *Scottish Journal of Theology* 41 (1988), pp. 177–89.

1989

'The Prophet Oded: sermon on 2 Chronicles 28.1–15', in *The Expository Times* 100 (1988–89) , pp. 383–4.

'The Grace of our Lord Jesus Christ: 2 Corinthians 8.1–9', in *Communio Viatorum* 32 (1989), pp. 105–9.

1990

** 'The Resurrection of Jesus Christ', in *The Expository Times* 101 (1989–90), pp. 167–72.

'God's Costly Forgiveness: sermon on Isaiah 53.6c', in *The Expository Times* 101 (1989–90), pp. 178–80.

** 'Giving a dog a bad name: a note on H. Räisänen's *Paul and the Law*, in *Journal for the Study of the New Testament* 38 (1990), pp. 77–85.

'One Dissenter's thoughts on the Book of Common Prayer', in M. Johnson (ed.), *Thomas Cranmer: essays in commemoration of the 500th anniversary of his birth*, Durham, 1990, pp. 229–39.

1991

'Guidance for Christians facing war' (letter to the editor), in *Reform*, January 1991, p. 31.

'A goodly heritage', in *Metanoia* 1 (1991), pp. 23–8.

** '"The works of the law" in the Epistle to the Romans', in *Journal for the Study of the New Testament* 43 (1991), pp. 89–101.

1992

'The effects of idolized market forces' (letter to the editor), in *Metanoia* 2 (1992), pp. 91–3.

'Dying with Christ and being raised with Christ (Colossians 3.1–15)', in *Metanoia* 2 (1992), pp. 99–102.

1993

'Self-denial: sermon on Matthew 16.24', in *The Expository Times* 104 (1992–93), pp. 143–5.

** 'Has the Old Testament law a place in the Christian life? A response to Professor Westerholm', in *Irish Biblical Studies* 15 (1993), pp. 50–64.

'Some human relationships: sermon on Colossians 3.18–4.1', in *The Expository Times* 104 (1992–93), pp. 305–7.

'The Parable of the Unmerciful Servant: sermon on Matthew 18.23–35', in *The Expository Times* 104 (1992–93), pp. 339–41.

The Apostles' Creed: a faith to live by, Grand Rapids and Edinburgh, 1993. A Japanese translation was published, Tokyo, 1995.

1994

'World Council of Churches too anxious not to offend the Serbs?' (letter to the editor), in *Reform*, April 1994, p. 24.

'With all thy mind: sermon on Mark 12.30', in *The Expository Times* 105 (1993–94), pp. 306–7.

** 'Who are Christ's brothers (Matthew 25.40)?', in *Metanoia* 4 (1994), pp. 31–9.

** 'Romans 6.1–14 revisited', in *The Expository Times* 106 (1994–95), pp. 40–3.

1995

** 'Paul's teaching on sanctification, with special reference to the Epistle to the Romans', in *Reformed Review* 48 (1994–95), pp. 217–29. Reprinted in *Metanoia* 5 (1995), pp. 194–208.

1996

'With confidence to the throne of grace: sermon on Hebrews 4.14–16', in *The Expository Times* 107 (1995–96), pp. 113–15.

Index of
Chief Passages Discussed

189

Index of Names